UNDERSTANDING
HEDGE
FUNDS

D0721046

UNDERSTANDING HEDGE FUNDS

Scott Frush

McGraw-Hill

New York Chicago San Francisco Lisbon London
Madrid Mexico City Milan New Delhi
San Juan Seoul Singapore
Sydney Toronto

This publication is designed to provide accurate and authoritative information in regard to the subject matter covered. It is sold with the understanding that neither the author nor the publisher is engaged in rendering legal, accounting, or other professional service. If legal advice or other expert assistance is required, the services of a competent professional person should be sought.

> —*From a declaration of principles jointly adopted by a committee of the American Bar Association and a committee of publishers.*

This book is printed on acid-free paper.

McGraw-Hill books are available at special quantity discounts to use as premiums and sales promotions, or for use in corporate training programs. For more information, please write to the Director of Special Sales, Professional Publishing, McGraw-Hill, Two Penn Plaza, New York, NY 10121-2298. Or contact your local bookstore.

Library of Congress Cataloging-in-Publication Data

Frush, Scott P.
    Understanding hedge funds / by Scott P. Frush.
        p. cm.
    Includes index.
    ISBN 0-07-148593-7 (pbk. : alk. paper) 1. Hedge funds—United States. I. Title.
HG4930.F76 2007
332.64'5—dc22   2006030956

To my grandparents

Contents

Acknowledgments

My sincere thank you to the instrumental people that helped make this book happen. First and foremost, a special thank you to my wife Christina for her unwavering support, time, and heroic patience. For their professional insights, thank you to Niel Avendano, and David Collon.

The people at McGraw-Hill have once again provided me with the platform and opportunity for my work and to all of them, I say thank you. In particular, I am thankful to Stephen Isaacs and Dianne Wheeler for their vision and commitment to publishing this book. Thank you also to Carol Cooper for her superb work in editing my manuscript.

Sincere thanks to my advisory board at Frush Financial Group for their driving force and masterful tutelage. Most of all, thank you to all of my clients for giving me the opportunity to not only do what I love, but also for allowing me to make a difference in your lives.

Scott Frush
Bloomfield Hills, Michigan

Introduction: Gaining the Investment *hEdge*

Hedge funds are clearly revolutionizing the way we invest and manage our wealth. Hedge funds are unique and distinct from more "traditional" investments, such as mutual funds and standard stock and bond portfolios. Hedge funds provide enhanced opportunities, greater options, and open doors to new possibilities for investors looking to gain an edge. From their distinctive style, to their distinguishing culture, hedge funds provide an "alternative" approach to investing and rightfully play the role of both return enhancer and risk reducer. Investors, the financial marketplace, and those in the hedge fund trade all benefit as a result.

Hedge funds are not a new investing phenomenon; they have been around since the 1940s with more basic forms in operation even before that time. However, one can argue that the hedge fund trade is still in its infancy and therefore in the early stages of widespread acceptance and recognition. In the past, investing in hedge funds was primarily the stage of the high net worth individual, but times have changed. Now with the wildly popular fund of hedge funds, opportunities for the masses are available for those willing, able, and ready.

The target audience for this book is novice to intermediate investors looking to gain a solid understanding of hedge funds. However, given the breadth of material presented in this book, those with advanced knowledge will learn new things as well. The single directive of this book is to explain in simple language and easy to understand terms the most important aspects of hedge funds and how best to employ them. As a result, this book will not get into the nit and gritty or complex mathematics of hedge funds. Those topics can be explored once a solid understanding of the fundamentals is learned. This book's primary emphasis is to deliver a solid explanation of hedge funds and how investors can pursue building a portfolio of hedge funds.

Reshaping Investing with Hedge Funds

Conceptually, hedge funds are easy to think about and understand. However, they are difficult to master since they employ complicated trading strategies with the possibility of using derivatives and leverage. The growing popularity of hedge funds is attributed to solid performance, attractive investment opportunities, more talented and greater expertise in the trade, and better support systems.

The best decision rests not in stand-alone hedge fund investing, but rather in investing in a hedge fund within a traditional portfolio. It is the entire portfolio that matters, not the individual components of the portfolio. Return is not rewarded at the individual investment level, only at the portfolio level. Return is fundamentally related to risk – perhaps one of the most important lessons of investing.

The hedge fund trade is comprised of many talented and skillful fund managers, many of whom are entrepreneurs in their own right and establish their own hedge fund companies. The vast majority of hedge fund managers concentrate on one particular style – tactical, event-driven, relative value, or hybrid – and limit themselves from working in another style. The specialized strategies that hedge fund managers employ provide greater access to markets and opportunities. Part two will explore more on the common practices of the hedge fund trade.

Hedge Fund Universe: The Big Picture

Throughout this book you will read about the different types of hedge funds in the marketplace. Hedge funds are defined by not only the investment style of the hedge fund manager, but also in the tools and strategies they employ and follow to generate profits. Unfortunately, some people in the hedge fund trade use the words strategy, style, and tools interchangeably to mean the same thing. This is not really the case as there are differences. As the hedge fund industry grows and matures, more standardized terminology will be used. Nevertheless, this book will use style to represent the guiding investment purpose of a particular hedge fund, be it tactical, event-driven, relative value, or perhaps hybrid. Strategy will be used to describe the specific actions hedge fund managers follow in order to profit within their investment style. Finally, tools (or tactics and techniques) will be used to describe the common everyday practices hedge fund managers use to implement their desired strategies. These tools include selling short, employing leverage, and trading derivatives. Chapter 5 will delve into tools of the trade in detail.

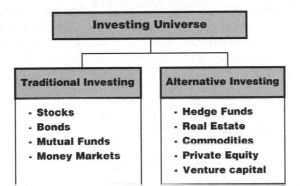

Figure I-1   Universe of Investing Opportunities

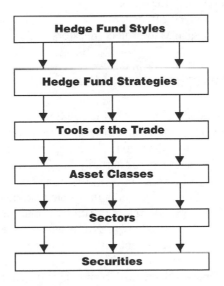

Figure I-2   Hedge Funds Universe

Defining Characteristics

Most investors are very comfortable and have good knowledge of traditional investing, particularly mutual funds. Practically all investors at one time or another have invested in mutual funds either on their own or through their employer's retirement program. In many ways, hedge funds operate the same. But they also differ in some key areas. Chapter 4 of this book breaks down the most significant differences between the more traditional mutual funds and the more alternative hedge funds. However, knowing what makes hedge funds, hedge funds, is an important first step. Presented below is a brief look at the top ten defining characteristics of hedge funds. Chapter 15 provides detailed descriptions of each defining characteristic and each is mentioned and expounded upon throughout this book at different times and in different ways.

- Small structure with one or two key people
- Minimal oversight and regulation
- Restricted to a low number of "accredited investors"
- Restrictive liquidity and redemption provisions
- Limitations on marketing and promotions
- Extensive tools of the trade
- Pursuit of absolute returns
- Low correlations with the market
- Dynamic fee arrangement
- Performance safeguards to protect investors

Leading Misconceptions about Hedge Funds

Before we begin our discussion of what hedge funds are, I thought it appropriate to discuss what hedge funds are not. This is sort of like separating fact from fiction and dispelling myth. The first misconception that many investors have is that hedge funds actually hedge something in particular, such as risk. Although this may have at one time been the single focus, it surely is not today. Many hedge funds do hedge risk, be it hedge fund-specific risk or portfolio risk, but the majority of hedge funds simply do not hedge risk. Many actually create risk. Not a big surprise to most people I suspect. The second misconception is that hedge funds take huge directional bets on a particular investment, notably global assets. Given the number of hedge funds in the marketplace, this absolutely is the case with a select few, but is not for most hedge funds. In reality, fewer than five percent of hedge funds are macro-centric, or the hedge funds most active in directional or tactical investments. Given the blow-ups with hedge funds and the media craze following them, this misconception is more or less understood. Third, many people have the notion that hedge fund managers love leverage and use it to the extreme. On the contrary, most hedge funds do not employ any leverage at all and those that do only do so under certain conditions, typically arbitrage conditions. Lastly, some people with little hedge fund knowledge assume that managers' use of derivatives is rampant. We have all heard about the hedge fund implosions, so derivative use must be great. Not true. The bulk of managers do not use derivatives at all or only for true hedging or safeguarding purposes.

Hedge Funds: Heroes or Villains?

Depending on whom you ask, some people will say that hedge funds provide a necessary function and role within the investing field. They say that hedge funds provide opportunity and have demonstrated solid success over the years. Given the safeguards put in place by hedge funds, by related brokerage firms, and by the regulatory agencies, hedge funds can only help rather than hurt. They are heroes of investing. However, there are some people who believe hedge funds are not heroes, but rather villains. They point to well-publicized hedge fund meltdowns as evidence. Once you do more research you will see that hedge funds do in fact provide more good than not. Some of the headline-grabbing hedge fund meltdowns of the recent past are as follows:

- *Long-Term Capital Management (LTCM)*: By far the most cited and most serious of hedge fund failures. Established in 1994, this fund placed large bets that were greatly impacted by the Russian financial crisis. Instead of liquidating positions, LTCM held their positions and lost billions, more than they had in total equity. A bailout from the federal government was needed to rectify the situation with LTCM unwinding positions in 2000. Chapter 2 on the history of hedge funds examines this debacle in greater detail.
- *Bailey Coates Cromwell Fund*: Although this London-based hedge fund was named Best New Equity Fund by Eurohedge in 2004, bad investments on the movements of U.S. stocks caused the fund to lose 20 percent of its $1.3 billion in assets. Soon thereafter, investors redeemed their capital and the fund closed by mid-2005.
- *Tiger Funds*: Run by legendary hedge fund manager Julian Robertson, this fund placed large investments in value securities and sold short growth securities during the bull market of the early 2000s. Although his

strategy was accurate, short-term momentum buying kept prices high and fund losses huge. The fund closed shortly afterwards.

Prudent and informed hedge fund investors know to do their homework about which fund or funds to hold and to never lose sight of risk. Moreover, prudent investors know to avoid hype and instead use common sense when making an investment. Part three of this book will help you to avoid the aforementioned scenarios of hedge fund failures.

Before We Get Started

Time and time again I tell people to manage your portfolio before it manages you. Managing your portfolio always begins with you. Never rely on someone else to do what you should be doing. When it comes to your investments, you really have two options; accomplish those tasks that will help you manage your portfolio or simply forgo them and let your portfolio manage you. Since you are already reading this book, you have demonstrated your ability and willingness to be proactive with managing your portfolio. Consider this book an invaluable tool to help you with your endeavor.

Self-Assessment

Before embarking on your endeavor of investing in hedge funds, I highly encourage you to complete a self-assessment. Since hedge fund investing is a personalized process and will change over time as your situation changes, learn as much as you can about where you currently stand, what you are hoping to accomplish, and how best to bridge the gap. Different investors have different goals and objectives and varying financial circumstances and preferences. As a result, care, skill and patience will be needed to reap the benefits of investing in hedge funds.

How to Get the Most from This Book

Understanding Hedge Funds is divided into four parts. No one part is of greater importance than the others. All parts are of equal value. Consequently, reading this book from chapter 1 to chapter 16 is your best route. The book is structured to provide maximum benefit, ease of learning and quick and simple referencing. As such, the book begins with a discussion of the essentials of hedge funds and is followed by a detailed discussion of the different hedge fund types, including common practices of hedge fund managers. Part three shows how to put into motion what parts one and two discussed to build your hedge fund portfolio. The final part helps to reinforce and enhance the first three parts and provides a view of what the future of hedge funds might be like.

A Review of the Chapters

Part one is all about the basics and theory of hedge funds. Chapter 1 leads off with an introduction to hedge funds and the key essentials. Chapter 2 provides a brief history of hedge funds from the inception to more modern times, including an examination of the Long-Term Capital Management debacle. This chapter examines the merits of investing in hedge funds. The third chapter emphasizes the role risk, return, and asset allocation serve with hedge funds, in particular the considerations for proper hedge fund investing. The final chapter in part one addresses the differences between mutual funds and hedge funds from the viewpoint of a novice hedge fund investor.

The second part of this book focuses on the different hedge fund styles and the tools that hedge funds managers employ to identify and take advantage of profitable opportunities. Accordingly, chapter 5 discusses the common tactics and techniques most common in the hedge fund trade. Chapter 6 follows this lead with a discussion of the most popular hedge funds, tactical hedge funds. These hedge funds aim to profit from directional price investments. Chapter 7 continues the discussion of hedge fund styles and presents event-driven hedge funds. Chapter 8 wraps up the stand-alone hedge fund styles by discussing relative value hedge funds. Finally, chapter 9 talks about hybrid hedge funds, which include multi-strategy funds and the very popular fund of hedge funds.

Part three begins the application phase for building a hedge fund portfolio. As such, chapter 10 kicks off with a discussion of the legal and regulatory challenges typically posed by hedge funds. Thereafter, chapter 11 presents ideas for conducting an effective hedge fund search. This chapter is appropriately followed-up with a discussion on making the initial hedge fund investment and how to make it work for you. The last chapter in part three explores how best to monitor your hedge fund and hedge fund manager.

Part four is all about some peripheral topics of hedge funds. Chapter 14 presents a brief look at how an investor can employ a self-manage strategy to manage his or her portfolio like a hedge fund. Numerous strategies are presented to accomplish this aim. Chapter 15 discusses the all-important top ten defining characteristics of hedge funds. And finally, chapter 16 gives a quick perspective on the future of hedge funds.

PART ONE

WHAT YOU NEED TO KNOW FIRST

1

Hedge Funds Explained: A Primer and Tutorial on the Key Essentials

Hedge Funds Tutorial

For investors looking to gain a performance edge, hedge funds could be the answer. Hedge funds are a powerful way for investors to build wealth. But what exactly is a hedge fund? In simple terms, a hedge fund is an actively managed private investment fund that seeks attractive positive returns. To accomplish this aim, hedge funds employ many different strategies, instruments and tools of the trade. Some strategies are aggressive and some are conservative. Hedge funds are managed by professional investment managers and are limited to a small number of "accredited investors." Hedge fund managers receive a percentage of the profits earned by the fund as an incentive to generate performance. Unlike most traditional investment managers, hedge fund managers usually have a significant amount of their wealth invested in their hedge fund. This minimizes conflicts of interest and gives a substantial amount of comfort to the investor in knowing that any results will impact both the investor and hedge fund manager.

Today, the use of the term hedge fund is generally considered to be a misnomer. Many hedge funds do not hedge risk at all, while many create more risk. The term was first introduced in the 1940s when Alfred Winslow Jones established the first hedge fund by employing long and short strategies enhanced with leverage. Since these early days, hedge funds have grown in both number and complexity. Although the type of hedge fund and their tools of the trade may have changed over the decades, the use of the catchy name has not.

How the SEC Views Hedge Funds

Although not statutorily defined by the SEC, the entity charged with regulating the securities markets and investment activities in the nation, statements made by the SEC provide a look inside on how they view hedge funds. The SEC has described hedge funds in the following ways:

> " 'Hedge fund' is a general, non-legal term used to describe private, unregistered investment pools that traditionally have been limited to sophisticated, wealthy investors. Hedge funds are not mutual funds and, as such, are not subject to the numerous regulations that apply to mutual funds for the protection of investors – including regulations requiring a certain degree of liquidity, regulations requiring that mutual fund shares be redeemable at any time, regulations protecting against conflicts of interest, regulations to assure fairness in the pricing of fund shares, disclosure regulations, regulations limiting the use of leverage, and more."

> —SECURITIES AND EXCHANGE COMMISSION, INVEST WISELY: AN
> INTRODUCTION TO MUTUAL FUNDS

> "Like mutual funds, hedge funds pool investors' money and invest those funds in financial instruments in an effort to make a positive return. However, unlike mutual funds, hedge funds are not registered with the SEC. This means that hedge funds are subject to very few regulatory controls. In addition, many hedge fund managers are not required to register with the SEC and therefore are not subject to regular SEC oversight. Because of this lack of regulatory oversight, hedge funds historically have been available to accredited investors and large institutions, and have limited investors through high investment minimums (e.g., $1 million).

Many hedge funds seek to profit in all kinds of markets by pursuing leveraging and other speculative investment practices that may increase the risk of investment loss."

—*SECURITIES AND EXCHANGE COMMISSION,*
HEDGING YOUR BETS: A HEADS UP ON HEDGE
FUNDS AND FUND OF HEDGE FUNDS

A Look at the Hedge Fund Industry

Hedge fund reporting service companies track anywhere from 4000 to 6000 hedge funds, although many experts estimate there are well over 7000 hedge funds in the world today, with some estimating over 9000. Many hedge funds are not tracked due to lack of size and thus do not show up in the numbers.

The hedge fund industry is dynamic in so many ways. Each hedge fund manager and more specifically each hedge fund will differ greatly. Some of the more important differences include size, composition, culture, performance, and strategies employed. Furthermore, these differences will change over time as the market fluctuates or a manager's objectives change. In an efficient market, change will create opportunities for growth and return. Thus everything remains in balance.

The hedge fund business has growth by leaps and bounds over the last couple of decades. For instance, in 1990 hedge funds managed nearly $40 billion in assets while 15 years later assets under management had grown to more than $975 billion, a head turning growth rate. Much of this increase in assets is attributed to new money, or cash inflows, with the rest of the growth from appreciation of principle. Net inflows of new assets into hedge funds have averaged in the high teens per year, with some years experiencing near 50 percent growth in assets. Today the growth rate in new assets is near 10 – 11 percent per year.

At the same time as assets were pouring into hedge funds, so too were new hedge funds being established to capitalize on the growth. Since 1990, the number of hedge funds has increased dramatically to near 9,000 worldwide with assets under management of approximately $1 trillion. Between 2001 and 2004, 612 new hedge funds were established on average each year.

Hedge funds and mutual funds differ substantially in the amount of assets they manage. There are some hedge funds that are quite large and some that are quite small. Typically, however, hedge funds are much smaller than mutual funds by a wide margin. Much to the surprise of many investors, there are numerous hedge funds with assets under management of less than $10 million and few with assets under management of greater than $5 billion. With hedge funds, smaller is considered more ideal as smaller means the hedge fund manager can take investment action much faster and without artificially moving the market as some mutual funds often do. In addition, smaller hedge funds allow managers to take positions in smaller investments whereas mutual funds cannot given that even a small investment on their part would equate to a large investment from a hedge fund, thus artificially moving the market. The performance incentive fee for hedge funds is established to support this kind of activity to capitalize on smaller investments. To further complicate the matter for mutual funds – and thus presenting opportunity to hedge funds – the SEC established a rule in 1998 that prohibits mutual funds from engaging in short-term trading and obtaining related returns. Hedge funds are not required to follow this rule, the so-called "short short rule."

Specifically, over two-thirds of hedge funds have assets under management in the range of $25 million to $100 million. As for the smaller hedge funds, or those with assets under management of less than $25 million, approximately 22 percent of hedge funds are represented here. The biggest hedge funds, or those over $100 million in assets under management, represent only a fraction of the total number of hedge funds at approximately 10 percent. Hedge funds with over $1 billion in assets under management can be considered "monster" sized funds. However, less than 5 percent of all hedge funds have asset levels this high.

The age of hedge funds is as varied as the types of hedge funds. Given the large number of hedge funds that have entered the field within the recent past, the vast majority of hedge funds, approximately 75 percent,

Assets Managed	% of All Funds
< $10 million	22%
$10 - $25 million	16%
$25 - $100 million	33%
$100 - $200 million	11%
$200 - $500 million	11%
$500 - $1000 million	4%
> $1 billion	3%

Figure 1-1   Hedge Funds by Approximate Asset Size

Age	% of All Funds
< 1 Year	14%
1 to 2 Years	16%
2 to 3 Years	15%
3 to 5 Years	18%
5 to 7 Years	13%
> 7 Years	24%

Figure 1-2   Hedge Funds by Approximate Age

have not been in existence for more than ten years. The newest hedge funds comprise approximately 15 percent of all existing funds, while the average age is in the three to eight year mark.

Hedge Fund Objectives

The primary objective for most hedge funds is to deliver long-term growth of capital. This is not always the case since some hedge funds may target other objectives such as a highly focused risk reduction strategy. Nevertheless, hedge funds typically strive to achieve a return that exceeds the rate of inflation over the period in question. Doing so will protect what is called real purchasing power, or the ability to purchase goods and services with a stable and specific amount of money. Depending on the hedge fund, the strategies they employ may be more aggressive while other strategies may be less aggressive. Protecting purchasing power without placing the portfolio at substantial risk is the aim no matter how risky the strategy. Hedge funds looking to accomplish this aim will invest nearly all of their assets in the U.S. stock market as well as international stock markets. Given the strong performance track records over time, the stock markets provide the best means to achieve this aim.

As with mutual fund managers, hedge fund managers also measure themselves against certain performance benchmarks. Mutual fund managers measure themselves against their peers and, as a result, attempt to deliver solid relative returns. Relative returns are returns that best other managers in their peer group. With hedge funds, managers measure their performance against other hedge fund managers; however, they place significantly more emphasis on what is called absolute performance or absolute returns. Here managers will attempt to deliver positive returns first rather than attempt to best their peers. Delivering performance that surpasses that of similar hedge funds is not the prime directive, only a secondary consideration to delivering positive returns. We will take a look at relative performance and measurement first.

As mentioned, relative performance and measurement is attempting to best your peers in performance. Little consideration is given to returns that fall outside the style and strategy of the manager in question. Comparing against a benchmark that tracks investments that are not in the same style or strategy as the manager is a fruitless endeavor. Comparisons must be made using apples to apples and oranges to oranges. For example, large cap equity managers will measure themselves against the S&P 500 while small cap equity managers will measure themselves against the Wilshire 5000. Doing so will give the manager and the investor a good look into the value the manager is creating or losing.

If a certain manager earns 12 percent when the passive index returns 9 percent, then the manager is delivering good relative performance. He gets to keep his job. However, if a manager earns a 6 percent return when the same passive index returns 9 percent, then the manager is losing value. Likewise, if a manager delivers a return of –4 percent, but the index delivers –7 percent, then the manager is still delivering good relative performance. With relative performance, no consideration is given to whether or not the return is positive or negative as long as it surpasses the return of the peer group, as measured by the index. Comparing a manager against a benchmark is a solid way to measure the value he or she is adding. However, in down markets a good relative performance can still be negative, and as we know, losses are still money foregone. You cannot fund your retirement with losses. Therefore, absolute returns and performance measurement provide a good way to evaluate and compare managers.

Absolute returns are returns that are positive, regardless of whether you earn a 25 percent return or a 1 percent return. Depending on the amount of risk a manager is willing and able to take, an aggressive fund might target returns of 20 percent annually, while moderate risk funds might target returns of 15 percent annually. Regardless of the degree of positive returns sought by the manager, simply earning positive returns is the primary goal of the hedge fund manager. Delivering a certain level of positive return is the secondary goal. Putting them together, the industry goal is to generate attractive positive returns. The more attractive the return the better, as hedge fund managers receive most of their compensation from a performance incentive fee.

To generate absolute returns, hedge fund managers will employ strategies and tools that take into account existing investments, such as treasuries. Consequently, one hedge fund manager may say that he wants to generate a premium to five year Treasury Notes while another manager may want to generate a premium to LIBOR, or the London Interbank Offered Rate. Given markets that move both up and down, generating absolute returns is not always a forgone conclusion. Thus, hedge fund managers will need to manage in such a way that the overall market does not matter. If a hedge fund is able to accomplish this goal, then they are said to be "all weather" funds. Regardless of how well the market does, these funds can weather the markets.

There is one final note on the use by hedge funds of absolute returns rather than relative returns. That being the elimination of a protective shield for hedge fund managers. When a relative return is used to measure performance, a mutual fund manager can use that to defend his or her track record even if the good relative performance is negative. Under this scenario, the manager still has lost money. However, hedge fund managers can not hide behind this shield. Hedge fund managers are charged with the goal of generating absolute returns, thus giving their clients more comfort in knowing the manager is looking after their investment with the best of intentions.

Performance Track Record

Over the last twenty years or so, hedge funds have performed quite nicely, particularly against the overall market as measured by the S&P 500. At the same time, the aggregate volatility in hedge funds was lower than that of the overall market. And lower volatility translates into less investment risk. When you dissect the performance of the market and the performance of hedge funds, you will find that the market outperformed hedge funds during the period of strong equity returns in the late 1990s to early 2000s. However, with the markets losing steam and equities falling precipitously, hedge funds began to not only make up the ground, but also to surpass the market in total return. This sharp move to the downside by the equity market was the primary driver of volatility and added investment risk, as compared to hedge funds.

What is more important than the absolute returns of the market and hedge funds is the number of months that each delivered a positive performance. During this same period, the market delivered positive returns about two-thirds of the time, while hedge funds delivered positive returns for nearly three-quarters of the time. Although the overall market did enjoy a higher average monthly gain over this time period, the market also experienced a higher average monthly loss over the same time period. With that being said, hedge funds outperformed the market on both an absolute return as well as a risk-adjusted return basis. The performance data clearly favored hedge funds in aggregate.

One final point to note about performance before moving on is that performance within hedge funds was varied depending on the type of strategy employed by the manager. Over any particular time period in question, one strategy may do well, while another may not. For instance, during 1994, merger arbitrage strategies delivered the best returns in hedge funds. However, the following year that same strategy would have underperformed many other hedge fund strategies, even though all were decisively positive. Hedge funds called funds of hedge funds provide a solid solution as they typically invest in a number of different hedge funds thus providing enhanced diversification. The end result is less volatility and a higher risk-adjusted return for both the hedge fund and the investor's portfolio.

Hedge Fund Risk and Return

Investment risk and return are inextricably linked. There is no free lunch when it comes to generating returns. If you want to earn a high return, you must accept a corresponding high risk investment. Any promise of a high return with little to no risk is a sure sign of investment fraud. Nevertheless, generating an attractive positive return is the goal. But what are the sources of risk and the corresponding factors that determine return potential?

With traditional investing, risk and return is determined by three distinct factors. The first is the performance of the market or asset class; the second is the investment strategy (asset allocation, security selection or market timing) employed to capture returns in a market or asset class; and the third is the skill of the investor or investment manager to implement, monitor and manage the strategy employed. This means that the return of a mutual fund is subject to the market or asset class performance, which is not typically under the control of the manager. Thus, the emphasis on relative returns rather than on absolute returns. In a traditional market, it is the strategy employed to capture the return of the market or asset class that is the leading determinant of portfolio performance. Study after study has proven this out. Properly allocating your assets is therefore the leading determinant of performance over time. Chapter 3 talks about how combining asset allocation and hedge funds can maximize your portfolio.

Given the ability of hedge funds to go both long and short, the performance of the market or asset classes is essentially removed. Thus, the two factors that determine risk and the corresponding return for the hedge fund investor is the strategy employed by the hedge fund manager and the skill of the hedge fund manager in implementing, monitoring and managing that strategy. Thus, the emphasis is on absolute returns rather than on relative returns. As with traditional investing, it is again the strategy employed by the hedge fund manager that determines the majority of portfolio performance over time. These strategies could involve selling short large cap stocks and buying Treasury bonds or buying small cap stocks using significant leverage. It is the selection of the strategy that is vitally important.

Hedge fund managers will want to go long, or buy an investment, in order to take advantage of forecasted price advances. Likewise, managers will want to go short, or sell an investment, to take advantage of forecasted price declines. Having the ability, or at least the opportunity, to profit when markets are either advancing or declining is what makes hedge funds so unique and attractive. As a result, hedge fund managers can take pride when generating solid returns for they exercise greater influence over investment decisions and actions that impact the performance of their fund. On the contrary, mutual fund managers are hand-cuffed on what they can do. Thus, they have less impact on the performance of their fund. That paradigm is simply the nature of the business.

Structure, Organization and Culture

In hedge fund lingo, a drawdown is a period that begins with a loss and continues until that loss is earned back and subsequent new positive returns are then delivered. As a whole, hedge funds have achieved solid returns over the long-term with low volatility, thus there are few drawdowns. The perfect mix. This translates into the optimal wealth preservation and accumulation scenario. As a result, allocating a portion of an investment portfolio to hedge funds can be a wise move.

Hedge funds assist investors with achieving their investment goals and objectives by placing those investors with investment managers who take advantage of market inefficiencies in varied and unique ways. The hedge fund structure provides investors with the means to pool their capital together and have that capital invested the right way by a professional manager. Obviously you will want to do a thorough investigation of a manager to ensure he or she has the talent to earn solid returns and meet your expectations. Pooling funds with other investors is not only ideal for them, but also for hedge fund managers as it gives them greater latitude in making investment decisions, in taking investment action and, best of all for them, in earning their keep, the performance incentive fee. This structure creates a win-win situation for all involved.

Hedge funds are legally organized in several different ways depending on where the hedge fund is located, what type of investor the hedge fund is targeting and what the hedge fund is attempting to accomplish. Given the desire to create a pass-through of gains and losses to investors – rather than pay taxes from the hedge fund itself – hedge funds in the United States are primarily formed as either limited partnerships, trusts or limited liability companies (LLCs). Offshore registration is also commonplace with hedge funds.

Structure

Under the limited partnership arrangement, hedge funds register with the appropriate state agencies, as all other limited partnerships are so registered. With a limited partnership, there is one general partner who is responsible for all of the decision-making and numerous limited partners. Limited partners are only liable to the extent of their investment in the hedge fund; however, general partners have no such protection and are thus liable above and beyond the amount of their investment. Limited partners are the investors in the hedge fund while general partners are the managers of the hedge fund that assume this role as either an individual or as a corporation. Many hedge fund managers operate as general partners through another company as a way to avoid the unlimited personal liability, thus only exposing themselves to limited liability given the company serving as the general partner.

Limited partners are only held liable for any losses to the amount of their investment, which buys shares in the partnership. These limited partnership interests cannot be sold to other investors, but can be sold, or redeemed, to the hedge fund partnership provided certain established guidelines are met and followed.

With offshore hedge funds, the corporate tax structure is typically employed. Although this form of legal organization provides taxation on the corporate level, this usually does not happen with offshore funds given where the hedge fund is specifically organized. Such tax-friendly havens as the Cayman Islands and the Bahamas do not tax on the corporate level. This provides the motivation and justification for organizing hedge funds offshore. Offshore hedge funds tend to consist of non-U.S. investors, although certain U.S. tax-exempt institutions do participate. Many hedge fund companies operate both an onshore, (U.S. organized),

CATEGORY	DOMESTIC	OFFSHORE
Liquidity	Less	More
Structure	As limited partnership	As corporations
Number of Clients Permitted	Limited number	Potentially unlimited
Accredited Investor Limitations	Commonly done	Generally none
U.S. Investors Permitted	Yes	Typically no
U.S. Institutions Permitted	Yes	Typically yes
Fixed Set of Regulations	Yes	No, depends on country

Figure 1-3   Domestic vs. Offshore Hedge Funds

hedge fund and an offshore hedge fund that mirror one another. This expands the client base, provides for additional hedge fund assets and keeps open the limited number of slots each hedge fund is able to provide to domestic investors in domestic hedge funds. Hedge fund assets remain segregated even under this scenario, however.

Approximately 80 percent of all hedge fund managers in the world work somewhere in the United States. However, only about 35 to 40 percent of all hedge funds are organized in the United States, with most registered in tax-friendly Delaware. Thus, 60 to 65 percent are organized outside the United States in offshore funds. The majority of the offshore funds are organized in the Cayman Islands, followed by the British Virgin Islands, Bermuda, Ireland and the Bahamas.

Registration	% of All Funds
Delaware	30%
Cayman Islands	28%
British Virgin Islands	10%
Other	9%
Bermuda	8%
Ireland	3%
California	2%
New York	2%
Bahamas	2%
Guernsey	2%
Luxembourg	2%

Figure 1-4   Approximate Domicile of Hedge Fund Registration

Hedge fund companies themselves also differ from company to company. However, the typical hedge fund company is significantly smaller and with flatter organizational structures than mutual funds. This design enables hedge fund managers to quickly and easily respond to changes in the market and the introduction of new information that can influence the price of a stock or bond. Some hedge funds are designed around one or two key people, thus making decisions even more robust. Mutual fund organizations are not designed with this flexibility.

Many hedge fund managers have quite varied and diverse backgrounds that provide hedge funds with highly specialized knowledge and experience. Most hedge fund managers come from an investment background while many come with an entrepreneur attitude. Their typical first foray into hedge funds is to establish an investment company, launch a hedge fund and invest a significant portion of their assets in their hedge fund. Rarely will you find a hedge fund where the manager, or general partner, does not have some stake in the returns. Oftentimes managers will manage assets of friends and family as the fund grows and gains exposure. When managers run hedge funds with their money and that of their friends and family, they have an extra incentive to achieve solid absolute returns. Generating returns is the name of the game for hedge funds and, in doing so, time and effort to market the hedge fund is minimized. Given hedge fund regulation, managers are hand-cuffed in the marketing and advertising activities they can do to promote their funds to prospects. That is one of the trade-offs with hedge funds. Mutual funds are not hand-cuffed by these same marketing restrictions and can advertise and promote much more freely, within certain bounds of course. On a side note, many mutual fund organizations are entering the hedge fund field and are training their traditional mutual fund managers on how to run a successful hedge fund.

Separate Accounts

Most hedge funds are formed as one big pool or account. All of the assets from investors are commingled in the one account and managed by the hedge fund team. However, on certain occasions, hedge funds will establish what are called "separate accounts" for large hedge fund investors, typically institutions. Institutions like this format because they are the only investor with assets in the account. This provides for greater access to the hedge fund management team and enhanced transparency and disclosure of vital information. Many hedge funds do not like this format as it means greater burdens on the hedge fund company. Some hedge funds will accept this relationship and some will require the assets be commingled with the assets of the other investors.

Investor-Manager Relationship

Investing in a mutual fund is quite different from investing in a hedge fund. Although there are many similarities, they are sharp contrasts. One of the primary contrasts involves the investor-manager relationship. With mutual funds, an investor becomes a client of the manager. The same cannot be said for hedge funds since the investor and the manager become business partners. Such is evidenced by the legal arrangement they enter into with the limited partnership. A mutual fund manager may have no material personal assets in the fund he or she manages. However, the hedge fund manager will have a material investment in the fund that sometimes makes the manager the single largest investor in the hedge fund. Furthermore, the hedge fund manager is encouraged to have no investments outside of the fund. Activities such as front running – where the manager places trades in his personal account outside of the hedge fund and then makes trades in the same security in the hedge fund to create favorable price movement are eliminated when all the assets are invested in the fund. Doing so will provide the manager with added incentive and the investor with added comfort regarding the pursuit of performance. This can be seen as investing alongside a star manager. The key point here is that investors should investigate the level of personal assets that the hedge fund manager has invested in the hedge fund. If a certain hedge fund manager is unwilling to invest in the hedge fund he or she manages, why would you invest in that same fund? You probably would not.

  In the past, the typical hedge fund investors were affluent individuals and families. This is now changing as the funds of hedge funds are open to the mass of investors given their much lower initial investment requirements. Previously it was commonplace to find the majority of hedge fund investors to come from inside the United States. However, that trend is changing as more hedge funds are established around the globe thus opening up opportunities to foreign investors. At the same time, hedge funds have become more enticing to institutional investors such as pension funds, insurance companies and endowments. Hedge funds are responding to this increased interest from institutions and disclosing more information on the assets held in the hedge fund and the strategies employed by the managers. This in turn motivates more institutions to invest in hedge funds creating a giant disclosure-investing circle. Given that institutions tend to be much larger than the average affluent investor, hedge funds are more than willing to accommodate them. This is not always the case, but holds true for the bulk of them.

The SEC places tough restrictions on how and to whom hedge fund companies can market their funds to potential investors. Given these limitations provided to investment companies, hedge funds aim to maximize the assets under management by establishing minimum initial investment requirements. The minimum typically ranges from $100,000 to $5,000,000 but the most popular range is between $600,000 and $1,000,000. More than 25 percent of hedge funds enact this requirement provision. Higher minimums also attract more qualified and sophisticated investors.

During the startup phase, most hedge funds have lower minimum requirements as a way to entice investment. However, as the hedge fund grows in both asset size and number of investors, hedge funds will raise the minimum investment and contribution amount to maximize the assets they manage. Some investors will be forced out to make room for new larger investors.

Much to the disappointment of investors, hedge funds typically limit, or restrict altogether, the amount and form of information on the type of assets in the hedge fund and the specific strategies employed by the hedge fund management team. Disclosure of information has become the latest crusade of the SEC against hedge funds and before long we will probably see a balance struck. Doing so will help investors make more informed decisions, enable better monitoring of hedge fund managers and, unfortunately drive up costs and level the playing field among hedge funds. The essence of Darwinism is surely alive and well within the hedge fund industry.

$ Investment	% of All Funds
< $10,000	4%
$10,000 to $50,000	8%
$50,000 to $100,000	16%
$100,000 to $250,000	18%
$250,000 to $500,000	18%
$500,000 to $1,000,000	29%
> $1,000,000	7%

Figure 1-5   Approximate Minimum Initial Hedge Fund Investment

Liquidity Considerations

For investors, liquidity refers to the timing and notice period they must provide hedge fund managers prior to redeeming their partnership shares. These notice periods are oftentimes required to give the hedge fund manager sufficient time to deliver the required liquidity for withdrawal. This could take anywhere from a couple of weeks to a couple of months.

Mutual funds and hedge funds differ in the degree of liquidity they provide to investors. Mutual funds are required to provide daily liquidity to their investors; however, hedge funds are not thus required. With mutual funds, investors can deposit and withdraw cash from a mutual fund quite easily. The same cannot be said for hedge funds. With hedge funds, there is minimal liquidity. Investors are only permitted to withdraw their cash at certain prescribed intervals. Some hedge funds only allow investments and withdrawals once per year or even once every couple of years. More flexible hedge funds allow for monthly or quarterly investments and withdrawals. The most common provision allows for annual investments and withdrawals. The same daily liquidity that exists with mutual funds does not exist with hedge funds. Given that hedge fund investors typically are wealthy investors, daily liquidity restrictions are not critical.

In the hedge fund industry there is a term that describes this lack of liquidity and restrictions on investments and withdrawals. This term is called "lock up". Lock up also can be the period of time new investors must wait before their investment is subject to the hedge fund standard liquidity provision.

> EXAMPLE: On December 31st a new investor invests $2 million in a hedge fund with a lock up provision of one year and a quarterly liquidity provision. On the following December 31st, the lock up period ends and the investment is now subject to the standard liquidity provision. On March 31st, the investor is then given the opportunity to make additional investments or make a withdrawal.

Some hedge funds will institute longer lock up periods to give investors the impression that the hedge fund is more private and exclusive than other hedge funds that do not have the same lock up period. The concept of the lock up is not necessarily a bad thing. Lock ups give the hedge fund manager the ability and freedom to employ typical hedge fund strategies that would otherwise be hampered given no lock up. These strategies include selling short, high leverage and more importantly in the case of lock ups, holding illiquid investments. Being forced to sell an illiquid investment to accomodate investor withdrawals could have a serious negative impact on the performance of the hedge fund.

Depending on the fund's offering memorandum, some hedge funds will deliver securities rather than cash to make payment to the investor. This is not commonly done, but is possible for hedge funds that hold positions in illiquid or private securities.

Lastly, hedge funds typically require holding back a certain amount of a withdrawal, commonly 10 percent, for investors who want to withdraw 100 percent of their investment. This is called the holdover provision. The 10 percent held back will be released once the end of the year audit is complete.

Strategies and Tools of the Trade

What makes hedge funds so unique and powerful? The answer is the strategies they employ. Hedge funds are managed by intelligent, hard-working people. They can employ complex merger arbitrage strategies or employ a simple long position strategy. Many traditional money managers also employ strategies and give them fancy names to bring them to life and attract investors. However, the flexibility of the hedge fund manager in the breadth and depth of the varied investment strategies available at their disposal trumps the traditional strategies. This does not mean that it is a forgone conclusion that hedge fund managers will outperform traditional money managers, such as mutual fund managers, but the opportunity to do just that is greater with hedge fund managers- with the opportunity for greater risk as well. Such strategies are called alternative strategies while the other strategies, used by mutual fund managers, are called traditional strategies. For example, equity market neutral is an alternative strategy commonly employed by hedge fund managers but is not employed by traditional investment managers. The SEC restricts mutual funds from employing alternative investment strategies.

Mutual fund managers will invest in stocks and bonds that they believe will increase in price. Besting an appropriate peer benchmark is the aim. Hedge fund managers, on the other hand, will typically employ alternative strategies either to leverage existing opportunities or to take advantage of new opportunities. These strategies can be complex or simple, with many somewhere in the middle. Most people with a cursory knowledge of the financial markets will have little problem understanding how hedge fund strategies work.

In the universe of hedge funds, there are four broad categories, or styles, of hedge funds, which can be divided into fourteen hedge fund strategies. The strategies hedge fund managers often employ will at times deviate slightly from the following strategies; however, these strategies will still resemble one of those in the broad style category. Combining strategies is also common. Regardless of the strategy, each has the aim of generating attractive to strong absolute returns. The following are the strategies employed by hedge fund managers, presented by style:

* Style: Tactical (sometimes called Directional)
    ○ Macro-Centric: Strategy whereby the hedge fund manager invests in securities which capitalize on the broad markets of both domestic and global opportunities. This is considered a "top-down" approach to hedge fund investing. The objective is to profit from changes in markets that are attributed to government and business influence and intervention. Investments are almost always broad-based in nature, such as playing FX movements or investing in market indices. Leverage is commonly employed here as well. Typical Risk: High to Very High
    ○ Managed Futures: Strategy whereby the hedge fund manager invests in commodities with a momentum focus, hoping to ride the trend to attractive profits. Managed futures are required to register as Commodity Trading Advisors (CTAs) and sometimes as Commodity Pool Operators (CPOs). These types of financial instruments trade on regulated exchanges, although some can trade over-the-counter (OTC) with banks and brokers. Typical Risk: High
    ○ Long/Short Equity: The long/short equity strategy is essentially named for the practice of going long or going short equity securities. This type of hedge fund is the most fundamental of all hedge funds and was established by Alfred Jones himself. Hedge fund managers will go long securities they believe will increase in value and will go short securities they believe will decline in value. These hedge funds focus on reducing total portfolio risk by minimizing overall market exposure. Many managers will even use a two-dimensional bet, which means they go long for a particular equity security while going short for an entirely different equity security. Thus, when the price of the long position rises and the price of the short position declines, then the hedge fund will profit on both positions. This of course could go the other way as well with the hedge fund losing on both fronts if the long position declined in price and the short position increased in price. Typical Risk: Moderate to High
    ○ Sector Specific: Strategy whereby the hedge fund manager invests in both a long position of equities together with a short sale of

equities or equity market indices. Hedge fund managers will typically invest in sectors they are familiar with and knowledgeable about, thus the name of the strategy. Hedge fund managers are attracted to certain sectors due to the growth prospects. Therefore, betting on the direction of the sector with a long investment will take advantage of growth opportunities. To minimize total market risk, hedge fund managers will sometimes sell short the market index, thus leaving the hedge fund exposed to sector-specific risk only. Of course, with sector-specific risk comes sector-specific return potential. That is what hedge fund managers target by using this strategy. Typical Risk: High

- ○ Emerging Markets: Strategy whereby the hedge fund manager invests in international markets with specific emphasis on emerging markets. These markets are estimated to offer solid growth prospects that are generally considered volatile with inflation concerns. Given that most foreign markets do not permit short selling, hedge fund managers will be limited in the hedging actions they can employ. Typical Risk: High to Very High

- ○ Market Timing: Strategy whereby the hedge fund manager invests in asset classes that are forecasted to perform well in the short-term. Rebalancing the asset classes is typically done to take advantage of price rotation in asset classes. Relies heavily on the skill of the hedge fund manager to time the entry and exit points for each investment. Previously used to take advantage of price descrepencies with mutual funds. Typical Risk: High

- ○ Short Selling: Strategy whereby the hedge fund manager sells securities short with the objective of buying them back in the future at lower prices. This strategy is employed when the hedge fund manager believes the price for a security is overvalued given present earnings or projected future earnings prospects. Investments can be made in individual companies, sectors, asset classes or the overall market, such as measured by the S&P 500 index. Typical Risk: High to Very High

- Style: Relative Value (sometimes called Arbitrage)

  - ○ Convertible Arbitrage: Strategy whereby the hedge fund manager takes advantage of perceived price inequality that offers low-risk profit opportunities. For instance, a hedge fund manager may invest in a convertible bond security and then simultaneously sell short the equity stock with the objective of locking in the spread inequality between the two. This strategy is related to a market neutral strategy. Typical Risk: Low

- ○ Fixed-Income Arbitrage: Strategy whereby the hedge fund manager purchases a particular fixed-income security and immediately sells short another fixed-income security to minimize market risk. The opposite can be done if the hedge fund manager believes a particular security is overpriced rather than underpriced. Typical Risk: Low
- ○ Equity Market Neutral: Strategy whereby the hedge fund manager buys an equity security and sells short a related index to offset the systematic, or market, risk. In other words, a securities hedging strategy. The objective is to capitalize on the perceived growth prospects of the equity security and minimize the risk of the market from driving down the price. Leverage is commonly used to enhance results. Typical Risk: Low

- Style: Event-Driven

- ○ Distressed Securities: Strategy whereby the hedge fund manager invests in the equity or debt of struggling companies at oftentimes steep discounts to the manager's estimated values. This spread between the estimated value and the present market value can be attributed to any number of factors, including the restriction of some institutions from owning non investment grade securities and the resulting oversale of these securities. These companies are typically presently in or facing bankruptcy or reorganization. Typical Risk: Low to Moderate
- ○ Reasonable Value: Strategy whereby the hedge fund manager invests in securities that are selling at discounts to their perceived value as a result of being out of favor or being relatively unknown in the investment community. This strategy is similar to distressed securities but places more emphasis on those securities with lower levels of default risk. Typical Risk: Low to Moderate
- ○ Merger Arbitrage: Strategy whereby the hedge fund manager invests in event-driven scenarios where there are unique opportunities for profit. These situations include corporate takeovers, legal reorganizations, mergers and leveraged buyouts (LBOs). Capturing the market price spread between an acquirer and an acquiree involved in an acquisition is emphasized. Typical Risk: Moderate to High
- ○ Opportunistic Events: Strategy whereby the hedge fund manager invests in securities given short-term event-driven opportunities. These opportunities are considered one-time events that offer strong returns. Multiple and rotating hedge fund strategies may be employed by the hedge fund manager to capitalize on such opportunistic events. Typical Risk: Moderate to High

- Style: Hybrid

    ○ Multi-Strategy: Strategy whereby the hedge fund manager employs two or more strategies at one time or different times. Depending on the aim of the hedge fund manager, two strategies may be employed with equal emphasis or three strategies may be employed where one strategy is given more emphasis. Overweighting or underweighting strategies is common as managers attempt to take advantage of opportunities. Typical Risk: Low, Moderate, High

    ○ Fund of Hedge Funds: Strategy whereby the hedge fund manager invests in two or more hedge funds rather than directly investing in securities themselves. This strategy provides enhanced diversification from the combination of multiple asset classes. This strategy emphasizes long-term performance with minimal volatility. Typical Risk: Low to Moderate

Some of the above strategies are used to take advantage of long-term opportunities while others are defensive in nature and can be thought of as simple insurance. Each strategy is discussed in much greater detail in Part II of this book. Each chapter in Part II discusses strategies depending on their risk and reward profile. Many hedge fund strategies will have greater risk than traditional stock and bond strategies. However, some hedge fund strategies will actually be less risky than even the basic stock and bond strategy.

One last thought on the strategies employed by both hedge funds and mutual funds. Even though hedge funds have the opportunity to engage in risky strategies, it is possible for a hedge fund to build a low risk portfolio that adheres to strict SEC guidelines and requirements. At the same time, mutual funds can be quite risky even though they adhere to each and every guideline and requirement of the SEC. Do not be fooled into thinking that hedge funds are always more risky than their counterpart, mutual funds.

Fund of Hedge Funds

A "Fund of Hedge Funds", sometimes called a fund of funds, is very much what it appears – a hedge fund that invests in other hedge funds. Funds of hedge funds create pools of capital and then invest that capital in attractive hedge funds. They are typically organized using the same limited partnership or limited liability corporation method as non-funds of hedge funds. Likewise there will be a general partner who makes all of

HEDGE FUND STYLE	STRATEGIES	CORRELATION	VOLATILITY	LEVERAGE	RISK
Tactical	Macro-centric, Managed Futures, Emerging Markets, Sector Specific, Short Selling, Long/Short Equity	High	High to Very High	Moderate	High
Relative Value	Fixed-Income Arbitrage, Convertible Arbitrage, Equity Market Neutral	Low	Low	Very High	Low
Event-Driven	Distressed Securities, Merger Arbitrage, Reasonable Value, Opportunistic Events	Low	Low	Exceptionally High	Medium
Hybrid	Multi-Strategy, Fund of Hedge Funds	Low	Low to Moderate	Low to Moderate	Low to Medium

Figure 1-6   Characteristics of Hedge Fund Strategies

Strategy	% of All Funds
Short Selling	29%
Equity Hedge	19%
Event-Driven	13%
Macro-centric	11%
Managed Futures	6%
Distressed Securities	5%
Convertible Arbitrage	5%
Sector Specific	4%
Emerging Markets	3%
Fixed-Income Arbitrage	3%
Equity Market Neutral	2%
Merger Arbitrage	1%
Market Timing	0%

Figure 1-7   Assets Under Management by Strategy

the investment decisions – therefore assuming unlimited liability – and limited partners who assume risk up to the level of their investment only.

Unlike non-funds of hedge funds, the manager will not make direct investments. Rather, these managers will invest in two or more hedge funds. The primary decisions each fund of hedge funds manager must make involves risk management issues, market analysis and direction, appropriate hedge fund strategies, and selecting hedge funds that are expected to generate attractive absolute returns. Good fund of hedge funds managers will develop a fund of hedge funds that will exhibit low correlations with the overall market, experience solid performance and have lower volatility. As a result, the hedge fund will maximize return for the level of risk the hedge fund will incur.

As with mutual funds that pool money from investors and provide enhanced diversification, hedge funds do quite the same. The fund of hedge funds manager will allocate to multiple hedge funds to enhance the diversification benefit. In addition, funds of hedge funds also provide investors with the ability to invest in other hedge funds that they would otherwise be restricted from investing given their high investment requirements. A fund of hedge funds pools it's investment dollars together and essentially becomes one investor, thus meeting the requirement to invest in other stand alone hedge funds. In addition, funds of hedge funds also give individual investors more comfort in knowing that they will not need to monitor one single hedge fund manager to ensure performance and proper fit. The fund of hedge funds manager will accomplish this task. Funds of hedge funds provide for greater hedge fund access, enhanced diversification to the masses of investors and reduced manager oversight. However, these benefits do not come free. There is an added cost.

The cost of gaining these benefits is an extra layer of fees. The first being the fees charged by the fund of hedge funds and the second being the fees charged by the hedge funds that the fund of hedge funds invests in. Some fund of hedge funds managers charge a performance incentive fee while others do not. Funds of hedge funds that do not charge performance incentive fees, or a reduced version, may offer excellent ways for investors to enter the hedge fund market without incurring high fees. Funds of hedge funds are quickly becoming the leading way for the mass of investors to take advantage of hedge funds.

The bottom line with funds of hedge funds is to do your homework on the fund to ensure that the extra layer of fees is offset by the two benefits – enhanced diversification and greater access to hedge funds with high investment requirements.

Management Fees and Performance Fees

Hedge funds typically charge two types of fees – an investment management fee and a performance incentive fee. In contrast, mutual funds typically only charge one type of fee – an investment management fee. With an investment management fee, investors pay a fee based entirely on the amount of assets being managed. Traditional equity mutual funds charge a fixed percentage fee of anywhere between 1 and 1.75 percent of the assets under management. Some will charge even more. Many investors will not see this fee being deducted from their account since it is deducted each trading day based on an annualized percentage. The price of the fund is thus adjusted for the amount of the daily fee. Charging a fee based on the size of assets under management is ideal for money managers since fee income will rise at a faster rate than will expenses, given increasing assets under management. The drawback of this arrangement to the investor is that the money manager may be more focused on gaining additional assets through new business than on generating solid performance. An unfortunate conflict of interest.

This potential disconnect is significantly minimized with hedge funds. Tying compensation to performance is thus emphasized. As with mutual funds, hedge funds also charge an investment management fee based on the asset-size of the portfolio. This fee typically runs around 1 percent, with some hedge funds charging a higher fee and some charging a lower fee.

Hedge funds add a new element to the traditional fee method in that they charge a fee based on how well your investment performs. This is called a performance incentive fee. This fee is rather standardized in the United States at 20 percent of the profits earned by the hedge fund partnership. This fee is charged annually. Some hedge funds charge quarterly and some monthly, but an annual charge is the norm. For example, if a hedge fund were to generate returns of 15 percent in a certain year, then 80 percent of that return, or 12 percent, will be earned by the investor while 20 percent, or 3 percent, is earned by the hedge fund manager. Again, this fee can be higher or lower, but is usually 20 percent. Funds of hedge funds will charge a lower performance incentive fee, if they charge at all. Performance incentive fees can be quite lucrative to a successful hedge fund manager and when the manager benefits so to will the investor since that means that his or her portfolio will have appreciated. This is a true win-win situation for both partners. Moreover, performance incentive fees highly motivate the hedge fund manager to be diligent in his or her research, make smart decisions, initiate wise investment actions and manage positions with the utmost care and skill.

There are two safeguards that hedge fund managers put in place to protect investors and make then feel more comfortable with investing in hedge funds and paying the incentive fee. First, some hedge funds will only charge incentive fees and participate in the profits if the return of the fund is above a previously specified hurdle. This hurdle can be the rate on Treasury bills or the LIBOR rate. Fund performance below a hurdle rate will not require investors to pay the incentive fee.

EXAMPLE: In year one, the Discovery Hedge Fund generates a 3 percent return but has a 4 percent hurdle rate provision. As a result, no incentive fee is charged. However, in year two the Discovery Hedge Fund generates a return of 20 percent. Since the return generated is higher than the 4 percent hurdle rate, then incentive fees are triggered. In this case incentive fees will be charged on the difference between the return generated and the hurdle rate. Here 16 percent (20 − 4 percent) will be used to determine the performance incentive fee.

The second way hedge funds protect investors is by instituting a safeguard where incentive fees are triggered only when new profits are generated. In other words, if an investor earns a profit that is only returning the value of the fund to a previous level, then an incentive fee is not charged. This is called the "high-water mark." Covering the same ground twice and being charged twice for profits that were gained, lost and regained is simply not appropriate. Portfolios must venture to new highs before new performance incentive fees are triggered.

EXAMPLE: In year one, an performance investor earns a 20 percent return on his $2,000,000 portfolio. With a 20 percent performance incentive fee, the investor will profit $320,000 for a total portfolio value of $2,320,000. In year two, the investor experiences a 10 percent loss, or $232,000 for a total portfolio value of $2,088,000. Since the total value of the portfolio is not above the previous high, or high-water mark, then no performance incentive fee is triggered. In year three, the investor earns a 25 percent return, or $522,000 for a total portfolio value of $2,610,000. Since the investor already paid performance incentive fees to a portfolio value of $2,320,000, only the difference between the new portfolio value high and the previous high is charged the performance incentive fee. In this example, the investor will pay a 20 percent fee on $290,000 in new profits.

Most hedge funds do not institute hurdle rates, however, most do institute high-water mark safeguards. Each hedge fund will detail how and when fees are charged in their offering and disclosure documents. Any fees charged are used by the hedge fund to pay salaries and expenses related to legal, accounting, audit, administration and operations.

Tax Considerations

Mutual funds and hedge funds are very similar with regard to tax issues. Both are considered "pass-through entities." This means that hedge funds themselves do not pay taxes, but instead pass all gains and losses to the individual investors. If certain requirements are not met, then individual mutual funds will be forced to pay taxes, but as you can imagine, this rarely if ever occurs. Hedge funds are not forced to pay taxes at the fund level.

The frequency and amount hedge fund investors pay in taxes depend on the specific hedge fund and, more importantly, on the type of strategy employed by the manager. The actions of the hedge fund manager to carry out each said strategy will also be a factor in tax consequences. For instance, hedge fund strategies that emphasize significant trading will typically result in higher capital gains taxes than will strategies where little trading is made. Capital gains taxes are incurred when an investment is sold at a gain. The two types of capital gains taxes are short-term, meaning gains generated within one holding year, and long-term gains, or gains generated from holding an investment for greater than one year. Short-term capital gains are taxed at your appropriate income tax rate, while long-term capital gains taxes receive a somewhat more favorable rate.

The other tax consideration to be aware of is the tax incurred on dividends and interest payments. This income is received from stock dividends and interest payments from bonds. Depending on the type of hedge fund, an investor may or may not be exposed to this tax consideration. Many stocks do issue dividends, so most investors will incur some taxes on current income.

Not only does the type of hedge fund make a difference in the taxes investors incur, but so to is the type of investor. Individual investors will have taxable portfolios, however, many institutions, especially those investing in hedge funds, are tax-exempt. Thus, tax considerations do not make a difference to tax-exempt institutions as they do not pay taxes. However, for the bulk of individual investors, you have to care about taxes as they can take a serious bite out of your earnings. It is not what you earn each day when all is said and done, but rather it is what you keep. If you didn't keep the return at the end of the day, did you even really earn it? Chapter 11 discusses taxes in more detail, as does chapter 12 on what to look out for when investigating hedge fund managers before investing with them.

Regulatory Considerations

Hedge funds are limited in both the number and type of investors that they can have by both the SEC and the well-known Investment Company Act of 1940. This act provides very specific guidelines as to what type of investor hedge funds can accept and the total number of these people it can manage money for. The act also restricted hedge funds from offering securities publicly. In 1997 this landmark act was altered to bring it more in line with current investment times. Prior to 1997, this act stated that hedge funds can accept no more than 99 investors, or accredited investors as they call them. To the SEC, accredited investors are individuals who have met the following requirements:

- Earned at least $200,000 annually in income for the past two years and have a reasonable expectation of doing so into the future
- Earned, with the spouse, at least $300,000 annually in income
- Has a net worth of at least $1,000,000 after excluding the personal residence and automobile

After many years, the SEC revised its requirements and thus provided another means for hedge funds to operate. These rules, which are in effect today, allow hedge funds to accept an unlimited number of qualified purchasers, if the following requirements are satisfied:

- An individual or family must have investments of at least $5,000,000

- A person who manages money for others on a discretionary basis must have $25,000,000 in assets under management
- A trust, as long as each trustee is a qualified purchaser
- A company, as long as the beneficial owner is a qualified purchaser

The new requirements also prohibit the offering of shares publicly. In addition, all hedge fund managers were required to be registered with the SEC, a provision struck down by the courts in 2006.

Reporting, Disclosure and Documentation

In the past, hedge funds reported the performance of their funds on a quarterly or annual basis. However, given the increased interest in hedge funds by investors, performance is now being calculated on a more frequent basis. This is an extra burden for hedge funds, but well worth the effort to gain ideal investors. Nevertheless, monthly reporting of performance is most common, although no standardized reporting is employed. The CFA Institute, the most prominent industry association for investment professionals, highly encourages standardization of performance measurement and analysis.

New potential investors will receive three different documents prior to investing in a hedge fund. These documents include the following:

- Offering Memorandum
- Limited Partnership Agreement
- Subscription Agreement

An offering memorandum, or sometimes referred to as a price placement memorandum or prospectus, is the primary source of information for the investor about the hedge fund. This document details such key points as the manager's background, risks involved, conflicts of interest present, limited partnership agreement points of interest, fees and charges, redemption provisions and how fees and charges are calculated. Other information specific to the hedge fund is also provided all with the objective of giving the investor more information to make a sound investment decision.

The limited partnership document is the formal contract between the investor and the hedge fund manager. This document outlines how the relationship will be structured – limited and general partners – and the rights and responsibilities of each partner. How the hedge fund is to be operated will also be fully documented in the limited partnership agreement.

The subscription agreement is essentially an application for an investor to become a limited partner of the hedge fund. This "petition" so-to-speak, requires certain disclosures from the investor to ensure that he or she satisfies the accredited investor requirements as established and mandated by the SEC. On this document an investor will find questions relating to annual income, total net worth, liquid assets, trading experience and risk tolerance. Each investor is required to submit a completed document along with a check for the initial investment, which typically is around $500,000 to $1,000,000 (significantly lower for funds of hedge funds). Simply accepting the application does not obligate the hedge fund to permit the investor to become a limited partner. However, if the investor is accepted, the initial check is invested into the hedge fund and a confirmation letter is drafted and sent to the investor.

Only onshore hedge funds have the limited partnership agreement as offshore hedge funds are not typically structured as such.

In the next chapter, you will learn about the quest for performance nirvana, specifically the history and merits of hedge funds.

CHAPTER 2

History and Merits of Hedge Funds: The Quest for Performance Nirvana

Origin of Hedge Funds

Hedging risk began in the 19th century when commodity producers and merchants began employing forward contracts to lock in prices and ensure the delivery of a standardized product. This was the forerunner of the modern day hedge fund.

Most investment professionals would agree that the first recorded hedge fund was established in the late 1940s by Alfred Winslow Jones, a 1923 Harvard graduate, 1941 Ph.D. graduate from Columbia University, and a journalist with *Fortune* magazine early in his career. During his days with *Fortune* magazine, Jones became a student of the financial markets and engrossed himself with its inner workings. While researching and writing an article in 1948 on the current investing landscape and on how hedging can enhance returns and reduce risk, Alfred Jones concluded that he could design a better way to manage money and achieve abnormal returns over time. As a result, in 1949 Alfred Jones established what many consider the first recorded hedge fund to take advantage of market swings, both up and down, to generate the enhanced returns and reduced risk that he previously wrote about. To establish this hedge fund, Jones pooled together $60,000 from investors, including with $40,000 of his own money. Soon afterward he was employing the very strategies he hypothesized would deliver returns in both up and down markets. The two primary strategies he employed in his hedge fund were selling short and using leverage. These are the very two strategies that many hedge fund managers use today.

His investment general partnership, A.W. Jones & Co. sought to take long positions in individual equity securities when the market was rising and to take short positions in individual securities when the market was falling. Betting correctly, regardless of the change in the market, would produce a positive return. In times of greater confidence in which direction he thought the market would move, Alfred Jones employed leverage – or borrowing from a brokerage firm to buy more of an investment - thus magnifying the degree of his long or short positions to ultimately increase return. Alfred Jones called the use of short selling and leveraging "speculative tools used for conservative purposes". In 1952, Alfred Jones changed the legal structure from the established general partnership into the more advantageous and commonly used structure of today, the limited partnership. About the same time as the change in legal structure, Alfred Jones introduced for the first time a performance incentive fee which he set at 20 percent of returns. Alfred Jones was also the first hedge fund manager to place a significant amount of his own money in the hedge fund he managed. Most hedge fund managers today follow these same two concepts – performance incentive fees and placing manager money in their funds.

Given his stellar performance track record, in 1966 *Fortune* magazine published an article on Alfred Jones and his hedge fund titled The Jones' That Nobody Can Keep Up With. The article praised Alfred Jones and his performance track record and revealed that his performance bested even the top performing mutual fund by 44 percent and the top five-year performing mutual fund of the day by 85 percent, returns net of fees. Alfred Jones' popularity skyrocketed. The *Fortune* article grabbed the attention and interest of numerous investors and investment professionals alike. The allure of earning ten to twenty times what they were earning in traditional positions resulted in 140 new hedge funds between 1966 and 1968. The Jones' hedge fund in one shape or another existed into the 1970s and continued its solid performance track record.

Although the Alfred Jones hedge fund is considered the first recorded hedge fund, it may not have been the first. Earlier and more basic versions may have existed. For instance, the father of value investing, Benjamin Graham was known to have established an investment fund in the mid-1920s. This would have given Graham the opportunity and motivation to employ hedge fund strategies, such as short selling, to enhance the returns of his value picks. Other investment professionals surely would have used some hedge fund strategies prior to Alfred Jones establishing his hedge fund. Such simple and common strategies included leverage and arbitrage, especially with commodities.

Hedge Funds Gain Momentum

By the 1950s, more and more investment players began to enter the hedge fund arena attracted by the greater flexibility and attractive compensation. At around the same time, legendary investor Warren Buffett became involved in hedge funds with his company, Buffett Partnership, Ltd. His hedge fund returned investors a 24 percent annualized return for the 13 years his fund was in existence. Prior to dissolving his fund in 1969, he used his new wealth to acquire Berkshire Hathaway, then a rundown textile company and risky investment. Today Berkshire Hathaway is synonymous with investing greatness. I find it interesting how a former troubled textile company became such a successful financial services giant.

By the 1970s, there were about 150 hedge funds in existence with assets of nearly $1 billion. However, most of the new hedge funds did not adopt the same two alternative strategies, selling short and using leverage, to the degree as did Alfred Jones. The new managers did emphasize the use of leverage, but declined on employing selling short. This decision exposed them to the impact of falling market prices, which happened in the late 1960s. Given that most of the hedge funds held long equity positions, more than 70 percent of the total value held by hedge funds was lost in consequence. Ouch!

Other investment players, who made names for themselves early in their careers by participating in hedge funds, include George Soros and Michael Steinhardt. Soros began his career in hedge funds at the same time Warren Buffett was exiting the trade in 1969. Soros' first fund was with the investment firm of Bleichroeder & Co. Nearly five years later, Soros left Bleichroeder & Co. to establish his own hedge fund, the well-known Quantum Fund.

Another hedge fund company, established by Julian Robertson, a former stockbroker with Kidder Peabody, gained substantial fame.

His hedge funds were named for the big wild cats with his signature fund so named the Tiger Fund. The offshore sister fund was named the Jaguar Fund. These funds gained him much fame and fortune and helped to produce many subsequent hedge fund managers. These hedge fund managers were appropriately called "Tiger cubs".

During the turbulent 1960s and inflation era 1970s, hedge funds began to gain traction with investors as equity and fixed-income returns suffered under the weight of weak economics. Hard assets, referred to as alternative assets in the world of asset allocation, performed quite well. This occurrence is relatively common during times of inflation and economic hardship. As trading in commodities escalated so to did the number of investment firms into the business. Within a short time, specialized funds, commodity pools and futures funds were established by the mega-brokerage companies to take advantage of the new trading phenomenon. Some of these investment professionals gave birth to CTAs, or commodity trading advisors. Early pioneers in this area include Paul Tudor, John Henry, Julian Robertson, Bruce Kovner, and Louis Bacon. Many of the initial trading strategies targeted stocks of companies that operated in the commodity space rather than purchasing the commodities, or physical product, outright. For instance, many early funds purchased or sold short the stocks of companies that mined gold rather than purchasing gold itself directly on a mercantile exchange.

Unfortunately, the 1970s also saw its share of hedge fund challenges. With the markets advancing in the late 1960s and early 1970s, many hedge fund managers reverted to long only positions and abandoned many of the common hedge fund techniques. The bear market of 1973 to 1974 saw severe hedge fund losses causing many hedge funds to exit from the business altogether. Hedge fund research company, Tremont Partners, concluded that there were less than 75 hedge funds in existence by 1984.

The Modern Era

As hedge funds entered the 1980s, the landscape began to change with inflation coming under control and the economy gaining momentum. This resulted in rising equity prices in both the United States and in global markets. Soon thereafter, hedge fund managers began to create portfolios without borders and opened their offerings to include global assets. At the same time, more standardized futures contracts began to emerge, as did the breadth and depth of the specific commodities traded. FX, or foreign exchange, trading of currencies gained momentum, as did bonds from developed nations across the globe. Hedge funds became a truly global business and the number of hedge funds soared. This resulted in less hedge funds employing the traditional long/short model and instead incorporating FX and financial derivatives such as futures and options. By the late 1990s, the same research company, Tremont Partners, recorded over 3000 hedge funds of various sizes, cultures, and strategies employed. Total assets in these funds amounted to over $380 billion.

The 1980s also saw the beginnings of one of the biggest cases of insider trading Wall Street had ever seen. Enter Michael Milken of Drexel Burnham Lambert, Ivan Boesky, and the emergence of the junk bond market including junk bond investing. Note that junk bonds are the less appealing title for what are commonly called non-investment grade bonds. The original purpose of the junk bond market was to finance the acquisition of distressed companies. The age of the leveraged buyouts, or LBOs, had begun. Unfortunately, these LBOs created significant conflicts of interest and before long Michael Milken and friends were accused of insider trading. To save their necks, Milken and Boesky pledged to stay out of the investment business for life. So ended their popularized careers.

Year	Funds
1990	530
1991	694
1992	937
1993	1,277
1994	1,654
1995	2,006
1996	2,392
1997	2,563
1998	2,848
1999	3,102
2000	3,335
2001	3,904
2002	4,598
2003	5,065
2004	5,900
2005	7,110
2006(e)	8,000 - 9,000

Figure 2-1   Number of Hedge Funds

One of the more modern inventions is the fund of hedge funds. This fund allows for greater flexibility in the number of investors permitted to invest in any one hedge fund. Investors no longer need to have Bill Gates type of wealth to qualify for investing in hedge funds. In addition to offerings to the masses, funds of hedge funds also offer enhanced diversification.

Since 1990, the number of hedge funds has increased dramatically to near 9000 worldwide including assets under management of $1 trillion. The time of the hedge fund has come of age.

Participants in Hedge Funds

Previously in this chapter we discussed the history of hedge funds and mentioned some of the leading individual figures helping to make the hedge fund trade what it is today. In this section, we will quickly talk about some of the institutional players that are central to the success and growth of hedge funds. The following paragraphs mention six institutions and their role in this trade.

Aside from typical high net worth individuals and families, many other investors participate in hedge funds. One of the largest such players is pension funds. These sometimes mammoth sized portfolios are always on the hunt for top managers and their destination often leads them to hedge funds. They have substantial assets and are therefore one of the top non-individual hedge fund investors.

A second investor in hedge funds is insurance companies. Although insurance companies generally take a conservative approach with investing to ensure capital is available to pay claims in the future, they also know the importance of proper asset allocation and therefore seek out return enhancing and risk reducing opportunities. Their search often leads them to a hedge fund manager.

The third type of institution active with hedge funds includes foundations and endowments. They too have traditionally invested conservatively, but recognize the benefits of allocating even a small portion of their portfolio to alternative assets, notably hedge funds.

Fourth, banks and related financial institutions are now becoming a bigger force in hedge funds and will continue to gain traction in this trade over the next few years. Some are establishing their own stand-alone hedge funds while others are pursuing funds of hedge funds. That brings us to our next and biggest contributor of assets to hedge funds, the fund of hedge funds. Yes, this fund is technically a hedge fund itself, but as far as where new assets originate and flow into single stand-alone hedge funds, funds of hedge funds are a major force. More importantly, funds of hedge funds are growing and growing quickly. Many financial institutions prefer this route when entering the hedge fund trade.

Lastly, many corporations are central figures in hedge funds. This is not a big source of funds for hedge funds, but does provide an ample amount. As with banks and other financial institutions, corporations' interest level in hedge funds will continue to rise.

Historical Performance of Hedge Funds

The following charts are presented to give you a better understanding of how well some hedge fund strategies have performed over the twenty-five years as compared to the S&P 500. You will also notice a chart with returns and standard deviations. Each simply provides another way of looking at the historical performance data. The performance data provided below is from Greenwich Alternative Investments. Other providers of performance data include Morningstar and Standard and Poor's. With hedge funds gaining momentum, more and more performance suppliers will enter the market making comparisons of different funds much easier. The end of chapter 13 examines hedge fund performance benchmarking.

Key Merits of Hedge Funds

Thus far you have learned about the essentials of hedge funds and the broad reasons for investing in hedge funds. Many specific factors underlying hedge funds support the idea that even a small allocation can generate solid results over time. But what are these more specific reasons? In general, hedge funds have outperformed most other asset classes over time. In addition, hedge funds offer capital protection, risk management, neutral market correlation, lower volatility, and help to build a more properly allocated and diversified portfolio. The following is a list and discussion of the key merits of hedge funds.

A Hedge Fund...

- Aims for Positive Returns in Both Rising and Falling Markets
- Minimizes Portfolio Losses and Volatility
- Offers Potential for Aggressive Returns that Far Outpace the Market
- Promotes a Diversified and Optimal Portfolio
- Delivers Access to Typically Underutilized Opportunities
- Maximizes Portfolio Risk-Adjusted Returns
- Enhances Portfolio Risk Management

CATEGORY	AVERAGE ANNUAL RETURN	STANDARD DEVIATION	SHARP RATIO
Aggressive Growth	19%	22%	0.9
Convertible Arbitrage Index	−1%	3%	−0.2
Distressed Securities	18%	15%	1.2
Emerging Markets	24%	28%	0.9
Equity Market Neutral Index	16%	8%	2.0
Fixed Income Arbitrage Index	6%	0%	33.2
Macro-centric	19%	20%	0.9
Market Neutral Arbitrage	13%	8%	1.7
Market Timing	18%	18%	1.0
Merger Arbitrage Index	5%	2%	2.7
Opportunistic	21%	16%	1.3
Short Selling	4%	19%	0.2
Special Situations Index	18%	13%	1.4
Value Index	18%	12%	1.5
S&P 500	13%	17%	0.7

Source: *Greenwich Alternative Investments*

Figure 2-2   Hedge Fund Performance by Strategy

Aims for Positive Returns in Both Rising and Falling Markets

One of the primary aims of hedge funds is to generate positive returns regardless of how well or poorly the market is performing. Thus, hedge fund managers strive for absolute returns rather than relative returns, the aim of mutual fund managers. This merit is important because the value of

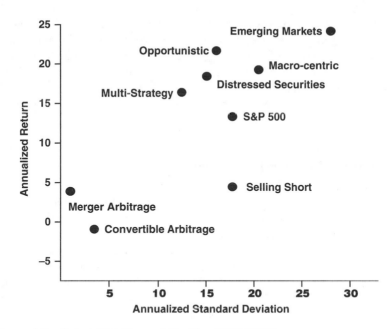

Figure 2-3   Select Risk/Reward Profiles (1999-2005)

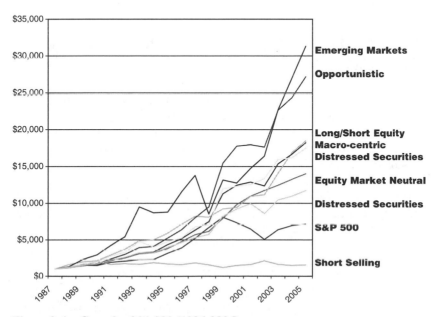

Figure 2-4   Growth of $1,000 (1986-2006)

your portfolio can be protected with greater ease. This is a significant consideration for investors who would rather earn a positive small return each and every year rather than have the possibility of earning substantial returns with the prospects of losing money when the market weakens. Hedge funds are uniquely positioned to deliver positive returns in any market because they can sell short securities. Thus, when the market falls, you will profit. This flexibility is a very important consideration for hedge funds.

Minimizes Portfolio Losses and Volatility

Nothing can devastate a portfolio like the impact from market crashes or prolonged market weakness. Over the history of the stock market, investors have experienced some crashes and numerous periods of prolonged weakness. At times, one asset class will perform well, while at other times another asset class will perform well. Hedge funds provide you with yet another investment option. By allocating to multiple-asset-classes, including hedge funds, which do not move in perfect lock-step form with each other, your portfolio will be shielded to a degree from excessive portfolio volatility. Holding a portfolio of only fixed-income securities typically creates greater portfolio risk than a balanced portfolio with both fixed-income and hedge funds.

Offers Potential for Aggressive Returns that Far Outpace the Market

Hedge funds provide the means to generate excessive portfolio returns. This merit is not to be confused with attractive performance over time. But rather, this merit is about hedge funds that can deliver substantial performance in the short-term. Most hedge funds are not organized to knock the cover off the baseball when it comes to performance; however, there are some hedge funds that target aggressive returns. Given hedge fund managers' ability to take advantage of less efficient markets and their freedom to move quickly with portfolio transactions, hedge funds provide the perfect means for those investors looking to take excessive risk in the hope of receiving excessive returns.

Promotes a Diversified and Optimal Portfolio

Each and every investor has a tolerance for risk as well as specific goals and needs. These goals are sometimes related to wealth accumulation, wealth preservation, or both. Once you identify your risk profile and specific goals and needs you are then able to design an optimal portfolio that can best achieve them. More specifically, you want to earn suitable portfolio performance over the long-term. Why is this important? It is important since many portfolios are designed with little regard for risk tolerance or goals and needs. You should never design or hold a portfolio that does not align expected portfolio performance with what you want to accomplish. A portfolio that aligns both your goals and needs and risk profile with expected portfolio performance provides you with your best chances for achieving them.

Hedge funds allow you to incorporate those assets that best matches your risk profile. By adding a hedge fund element to your portfolio, you will effectively create a more optimal portfolio. At the same time, given that hedge funds typically have more than one investment, portfolio diversification is also enhanced.

Delivers Access to Typically Underutilized Opportunities

There are many strategies for managing a portfolio. One way is to employ a mutual fund to do the job. This may or may not be a good approach. The true downside of mutual funds is in their restrictions on which strategies they are permitted to employ. Hedge funds do not have these same restrictions. As a result, your hedge fund manager is free to utilize many strategies to take advantage of profitable opportunities. Employing merger arbitrage and convertible arbitrage are two very good examples. Mutual fund managers cannot use these tools while most investors will not have the knowledge or skill to execute these as well. Thus, it is the hedge fund manager that provides the expertise and tools needed to employ these strategies. This equates to greater opportunities to enhance return and reduce risk in your portfolio.

Maximizes Portfolio Risk-Adjusted Return

Modern portfolio theory says that when an investor is faced with two investments with identical expected returns, but different levels of risk, he or she should select the investment that has the lower risk. Said from a different way, a rational investor will select the investment with the higher return when faced with two investments that have different expected returns but identical levels of risk. By combining

investments with different returns and risk levels, you will build a portfolio that provides the maximum risk-adjusted return. Hedge funds can
do just this.

The aim of hedge funds is to deliver attractive positive returns, or
what are called absolute returns. To accomplish this aim, hedge fund
managers need to develop funds that have low correlations, or neutral
correlations, to the overall market. Thus, when the market is rising or
falling, funds do not follow suit. This means that your level of portfolio
risk will decline and the potential for returns increase. In aggregate, the
risk-adjusted return of your portfolio will become more attractive.

Enhances Portfolio Risk Management

Protecting your portfolio and keeping risk under control is vitally
important to become a successful hedge fund investor. Given the complexity and tools necessary to manage a portfolio using alternative
strategies, investors will find it beneficial to leave this task to a professional. Hedge fund managers are well versed on the investing marketplace and how best to profit from it. At the same time, hedge fund
managers are experts at assessing risk and minimizing that risk as best
as possible. Most hedge funds are all about reducing portfolio risk,
rather than generating excessive returns. One of the best ways to reduce
risk is by incorporating investments that have neutral correlations to
the market. This is a specialty of many hedge fund managers. Hedge
funds provide the ability and opportunities to reduce portfolio risk
more than any other investment.

CATEGORY	ADVANTAGES	DISADVANTAGES
Absolute Return	Potential to outperform in bear markets	Probability of underperforming in bull markets
Alternative Strategies	Extensive Manager Freedom	Shifts risk from market to manager specific
Structure	Quick and easy decisions	Fewer thoughts on the issue at hand
Fee Charged	Promotes performance over growth of assets	Incentive to take extra risk on occasion
Liquidity	Fewer daily or weekly burdens	Turn-off potential clients

Figure 2-5   Hedge Fund Advantages and Disadvantages

Pitfalls Abound with Hedge Funds

Let's, examine some of the drawbacks of hedge funds. Each of these drawbacks is explored in greater depth throughout this book.

The first drawback of hedge funds is the issue of underperforming the market when the market is advancing. Since the most important aim of hedge funds is to deliver absolute returns, hedge funds are not always in a position to take advantage of market moves upward. This is attributed to a hedge fund holding short positions that offset long positions when the market moves higher. Nevertheless, hedge fund managers strive to deliver positive performance when the market is advancing, but may lag slightly.

The second drawback is the substantial manager-specific risk. Both traditional and alternative portfolios have inherent manager-specific risks; however, hedge funds will typically try to minimize market risk, thus leaving a fund with only manager-specific risk and company-specific-risk. The more any one risk is hedged the more emphasis is placed on the manager-specific risk. If the investment works out as anticipated then all is well.

But if the manager makes a poor decision, then the fund will lose.

Third, hedge funds typically are run by one or two key people. This is ideal when hedge funds want to make quick and easy investing decisions, but not so ideal when one of them leaves the company.

The fourth drawback is the incentive hedge fund managers have to take more risk to earn higher returns, and thus higher fees. Earning 20 percent of profits is definitely enticing to hedge fund managers and at some point he or she may be tempted to take slightly more risk than ordinarily taken.

Lastly, investors in hedge funds are confronted with unique challenges not generally seen with traditional investing. These challenges include a lack of liquidity and a lack of transparency. For investors that like to be in control, hedge funds may prove to be rather frustrating. These are more cosmetic issues, but are still important considerations that should be investigated prior to making the initial investment.

Long-Term Capital Management Debacle

Founded in Greenwich, Connecticut in 1994, Long-Term Capital Management (LTCM) was a hedge fund established by John Meriwether, the former vice-chairman and head of bond trading at Salomon Brothers. In addition to Meriwether, other founders included two 1997 Nobel

Prize-winning economists, Myron Scholes and Robert C. Merton. Scholes and Merton, together with the late Fischer Black, developed the Black-Scholes formula for option pricing. Also part of the team was David Mullins, a former vice chairman of the Board of Governors of the Federal Reserve System. Rounding out the team were many important arbitrage analysts from Salomon Brothers. The group was definitely very elite.

The minimum investment was originally set at $10 million with Merrill Lynch coordinating the financing. The legal structure involved the establishment of two partnerships, Long-Term Capital Portfolio in the Cayman Islands (the owner of record for the securities held) and Long-Term Capital Management (a Delaware company) managed in Connecticut. Contrary to the typical hedge fund, the LTCM fund charged a performance incentive fee of 25 percent (rather than 20 percent) and assessed a 2 percent asset-based fee (rather than 1 to 2 percent). Finally, LTCM implemented a three year lock-up period where the standard is one year.

On February 24, 1994, Long-Term Capital Management began trading with an asset base of $1,011,060,243. The strategy of the hedge fund was to hunt for and identify arbitrage opportunities in markets using computers, massive databases, and the forecasts of top level analysts. More specifically, LTCM had developed sophisticated and complex mathematical models with the aim of taking advantage of fixed-income arbitrage opportunities (termed convergence trades) typically with American, European, and Japanese government bonds. In essence, the thought was that over time the value of long-dated government bonds, issued together around the same date, would be approximately the same. Given the liquidity and heavy trading activity, U.S. Treasury bonds could approach the long-term price more quickly than the otherwise less heavily traded and less liquid government bonds from Europe and Japan. In hedge fund speak; this amounted to buying the cheaper "off-the-run" bond and selling short the more expensive, but more liquid, "on-the-run" bond.

The ideal opportunities came from markets that deviated from normal patterns and were likely to re-adjust to the normal patterns over time. By establishing hedged positions, the risks inherent in the market would be minimized to the lowest possible levels. This was the major flaw in the model developed by Robert C. Merton. Although the model assumed very low risk levels, in practice some of the vital model inputs and assumptions did not hold as anticipated. As a result, the risk of the hedged portfolios was not really zero, as subsequent events unfortunately proved out. Myron Scholes was known for expressing this aim as a giant vacuum cleaner sucking up nickels that everyone else had overlooked.

Long-Term Capital Management became an overnight success. In 1996, the firm generated a mind-boggling $2.1 billion profit. The secret wasn't that its investments highly appreciated in value. Rather, it was the staggering amounts of leverage that it employed. The firm earned a pity 1 to 2 percent return on its bets, but given the significant leverage, turned the pity profits into substantial profits. At its peak, Long-Term Capital Management had equity of $4.72 billion, borrowed funds of over $124.5 billion, and asset positions of $129 billion. In addition, Long-Term Capital Management held off-balance sheet derivative positions totaling $1.25 trillion, the majority of which included interest rate derivatives. This asset level made them two and a half times the size of Fidelity Magellan, one of the largest mutual funds at that time.

Everything stopped in 1998 when the Russian government defaulted on their government bonds (GKOs) in August and September. Nervous global investors sold their Japanese and European bonds and purchased U.S. Treasury bonds, a flight to liquidity. The profits that Long-Term Capital Management expected as the value of these bonds converged became huge losses as the value of the bonds diverged. This flight to liquidity led to a global repricing of all risk. Rather quickly, the correlation of LTCMs positions increased and the diversified aspect of their fund vanished with large resulting losses. By the end of August, the hedge fund had lost a whopping $1.85 billion in capital and was in danger of defaulting on its loans. Given the size of the loss, it was extremely difficult for the hedge fund to cut its losses. This is understandable since Long-Term Capital Management held huge positions, roughly 5 percent of the total global fixed-income market.

With substantial losses of capital by Long-Term Capital Management racking up, the banks that had provided the borrowed money for it to leverage became worried about the security of their loans. With Long-Term Capital Management on the brink of total failure and collapse, to the rescue came the Federal Reserve Bank of New York who brokered a bailout of the hedge fund. Fourteen major banks contributed nearly $300 million each to establish a $3.625 billion bailout loan fund. This fund, together with the remaining assets held by the hedge fund, allowed it to make it through the 1998 global financial crisis. This group of banks and the Fed reorganized Long-Term Capital Management and allowed it to operate for the single purpose of liquidating positions.

The hedge fund repaid all creditor banks and was completely liquidated in early 2000. In total, Long-Term Capital Management generated losses of about $4.6 billion, a feat done in less than four months. The losses included the following:

- $1,600 million in swaps
- $1,300 million in equity volatility

- $430 million in Russian and other emerging market debt
- $371 million in directional trades in developed countries
- $215 million in yield curve arbitrage
- $203 million in S&P 500 equities
- $100 million in junk bond arbitrage

If Long-Term Capital Management had gone into default, a more intense global financial crisis may have occurred leading to a chain reaction as the company liquidated its securities to cover its debt. For the sake of the financial markets, the situation was addressed quickly and resolved. Believe it or not, but John Meriwether and his team recently launched a new hedge fund called JWM Partners. The initial funding was approximately $250 million and pooled from former investors of Long-Term Capital Management. Strange twist of fate.

In the next chapter, you will learn about risk, return, and asset allocation, concepts that are important considerations for hedge fund investing.

3

Risk, Return, and Asset Allocation: Considerations for Hedge Fund Investing

No book on hedge funds would be complete without a chapter on risk, return, and asset allocation. The relationship between risk and return is central to the investing decision framework. This relationship essentially says that to earn higher level of returns, investors need to assume higher levels of risk. There is simply no other way to accomplish this aim. In addition, investors looking to assume low levels of risk will in aggregate earn lower risk. Asset allocation is very much related to risk and return and the relationship they play in portfolio construction. Hedge funds should not be approached as a stand-alone single investment. Rather, they should be approached as part of the overall picture, a component of asset allocation. It is for this reason that we dedicate this chapter to understanding asset allocation, including risk and return. For a more detailed discussion of asset allocation, please pick up your copy of *Understanding Asset Allocation*.

Asset allocation is founded on two celebrated and highly influential investment theories. They are the modern portfolio theory (MPT) and the efficient market hypothesis (EMH), which is essentially a refinement of MPT. These two theories are the most discussed and most widely used theories in all of investment management. You cannot pick up any book on hedge funds without reading about discussions on the risk-reward profile of individual hedge fund strategies. Those discussions provide charts and graphs and typically incorporate sharp ratios. All of these are directly related to both of the aforementioned theories.

The modern portfolio theory says that investors and portfolio managers should not evaluate each investment on a standalone basis. Rather, each investment should be evaluated based on its ability to enhance the overall risk and return profile of a portfolio. When faced with two investments with identical expected returns but different levels of risk, investors should select the investment that has the lower risk according to the modern portfolio theory. Said from another approach, a rational investor will select the investment with the higher return when faced with two investments that have different expected returns but identical levels of risk.

When faced with investments A and B, a rational investor will select investment B over investment A because the total return of investment B is higher, with both having the same level of risk. Moreover, when faced with investments B and C, a rational investor will select investment C over investment B because the total risk of investment C is lower, with

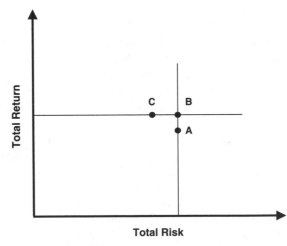

Source: Frush Financial Group

Figure 3-1   Investment Alternatives and Rational Decisions

both having the same total return. Pretty simple stuff, but it was revolutionary when first put forth.

Lastly, modern portfolio theory introduces the concept of correlation and stresses how it enhances the risk and return profile of a portfolio. The Employee Retirement Income Security Act of 1974, which governs the management of pension funds, emphasizes this point, thus essentially endorsing MPT. Harry M. Markowitz, who was awarded the Noble Prize in Economics in 1990, is considered the "father of modern portfolio theory" for this work.

Understanding Correlation

An optimal portfolio is not just the sum of its parts. Rather, an optimal portfolio is the sum of its synergies. Synergies are created by the interaction of the investments held within a portfolio. This interaction is commonly referred to as correlation and is a critical input to the asset allocation process. Correlation is the technical term used to measure and describe how closely the prices of two investments move together over time.

Positively correlated assets move in the same direction, both up and down. Conversely, negatively correlated assets move in opposite directions. Correlations between two assets are expressed on a scale between –1.0 and +1.0. The greater two assets are correlated, or move together, the closer to +1.0. Similarly, the greater two assets move in opposite directions, the closer to –1.0. Two assets that move exactly together have a +1.0 correlation while two assets that move exactly opposite have a –1.0 correlation.

> EXAMPLE: The correlation between Stock A and Stock B is 0.8. As a result, for every $1 price movement in either stock, the other will move 80 percent in the same direction over the same time period.

Correlations between –0.3 and +0.3 are thought to be non-correlated. This means that the two asset classes move independently of each other. With non-correlated assets, when one is rising in price, the other may be rising, falling, or maintaining its current price.

A properly allocated portfolio has a mix of investments that do not behave the same way. Correlation is therefore the measure you need to be concerned about. To maximize the portfolio benefits derived from correlations, you will need to incorporate investments with negative correlations, low positive correlations, or even assets that have non-correlations.

Figure 3-2   Spectrum of Hedge Fund Correlation

Non-correlated investments move independently from each other. By investing in assets with low correlations, you are able to reduce total portfolio risk without impacting the return of your portfolio. Doing so will help to greatly minimize the overall investment-specific risk attributed to each investment.

The greatest portfolio risk reduction benefits occur during time periods when correlations across the board are low, non-correlated, or negative. When correlations increase, risk reduction benefits are partially lost. Over time, some correlations will increase and some will decline.

Since you cannot predict which correlations will change, or to what degree they will change, over time, successful investors will allocate to a number of fundamentally different investments to reap the benefits of asset allocation.

Time Horizon Explained

Your time horizon is another very important input variable. Most investors pay too little attention to time horizon and the important role it plays. Your time horizon impacts expected rates of return, expected volatility, and expected investment correlations.

As a result of the important role it plays, time horizon is the first constraint that should be identified. Overestimating or underestimating your time horizon can significantly impact how you allocate your assets and thereby impacting your risk and return profile.

The primary role time horizon plays is to help you select and evaluate the appropriateness of each asset class and asset subclass as an investment alternative. Specifically, time horizon helps to determine your balance between equity investments and fixed-income investments. The shorter your time horizon the more emphasis you should place on fixed-income investments. Conversely, the longer your time horizon the more emphasis you should place on equity investments. In the short-term, equities are simply too volatile and possess high levels of uncertainty. Said another way, equities exhibit unacceptable levels of risk in relation to their expected returns. On the other hand, fixed-income investments are significantly less volatile in the short-term and possess much lower levels of uncertainty. As a consequence, fixed-income risks in relation to their expected returns are more favorable in the short-term.

As your investment time horizon increases, so too does the probability of your equity assets experiencing positive returns. Over longer periods of time equity returns become more stable as there is more time for positive equity returns to offset negative equity returns. The returns of equities become significantly more clear and predictable as your investment time horizon lengthens.

Risk and Return

No one particularly likes risk. Furthermore, no one particularly likes risk when risk becomes reality and befalls misfortune. Avoiding risk is therefore highly ideal. However, doing so is not entirely feasible in the world of investing since there is a clear and profound relationship between risk and return. Risk is an inherent part of any investment undertaking making it critical to understand this inescapable trade-off. Getting blindsided by the realization of risk needs to be evaluated when making investment decisions. So too does the potential for strong returns.

Unfortunately, we hear the very opposite practically every day in nearly all places that reward can be earned with little to no risk. Reward without risk does not exist in the investment marketplace. Don't let anyone tell you otherwise. Abnormally high returns are not uncommon, but they are neither predictable, nor consistent over time. Consequently, if you desire a return that outpaces both inflation and taxes, then you must be prepared to assume some level of risk. You get what you pay for and earn what you invest in. As you know, you do not get something for nothing.

Two of the most important concepts an investor should learn and fully understand are investment return and investment risk. These two concepts and how they work together are the foundations of asset allocation and its application to building an optimal portfolio. Depending on your objectives and constraints, you may invest in assets that exhibit low risk and therefore the potential for low, but stable returns, or you may invest in assets that exhibit high risk and therefore the potential for high, but oftentimes, volatile returns. In basic asset allocation theory, the higher the potential risk you take, the higher the potential return you should earn. Moreover, rational investors will not assume a higher level of risk in the hopes of earning a return that another investment may earn, but with a lower level of risk.

The million-dollar question is how to enhance your returns and still avoid risk. Although risk cannot be entirely eliminated from a portfolio, it can be controlled and managed with a proper asset allocation policy. A portfolio that is optimally designed, built and managed will exhibit a higher risk-adjusted return than portfolios not subscribing to proper asset allocation, regardless of having high return investments in that portfolio.

Investment Risk

Investment risk can be defined in many different ways and investors view risk differently from other investors. Some investors define risk as losing money, while others define risk as unfamiliar investments. Still others define risk as contrarian risk, or the risk investors feel when they are not "following the crowd." If you were to toss out all of the subjective definitions, risk is defined more objectively as uncertainty, or the uncertainty that actual investment returns will equal expected returns. Pension funds and insurance companies view risk as the uncertainty they can meet future benefit obligations while mutual funds view risk as underperforming peer mutual funds and/or an industry benchmark, such as the S&P 500. As for individual investors, they tend to view risk as losing money in their portfolios, whether that loss is temporary or permanent. This may not be the best method for viewing risk, but it is the most understood and applied by individual investors.

In aggregate, most investment experts define risk quite rigidly as the volatility of returns over a specific time period. Most risk measurements are accomplished using monthly price movements for individual securities, whether those movements are up or down. The greater the monthly movement, regardless of direction, the larger the volatility measure and therefore the greater the risk. Volatility also impacts total performance.

Portfolios with more volatility will exhibit lower long-term compounded growth rates of return. Thus, it is essential to minimize volatility in your portfolio for maximum appreciation over time.

Risk management and proper asset allocation reduce both the frequency and the amount of portfolio losses. Since you rely on estimates of future returns to design your optimal portfolio, it is critically important that actual returns come close to matching expected returns. Investments with more predictable returns are considered lower risk. Conversely, investments with less predictable returns are considered higher risk. Risk in one word can be called uncertainty. More specifically, the uncertainty that actual returns will match expected returns.

Asset Classes and Risk

Different asset classes possess different types and different amounts of risk, and therefore different expected returns. Each type of risk is derived from one or more sources of risk. Regardless of the type and source of investment risk, asset allocation will allow you to control and manage your risk exposure to the best of your advantage. Asset allocation is the key to total risk-reduction.

As previously mentioned, however, it is simply not enough to focus on the merits of one particular investment since it is how each investment moves in relation to the other investments that truly matters. Regardless of the risk and return potential for each asset, keep in mind that understanding their fundamentals and how they impact a portfolio is most important.

Sources of Investment Risk

There are two primary sources of risk. The first is called systematic risk, or risk attributed to relatively uncontrollable external factors. The second is called unsystematic risk, or risk attributed directly to the underlying investment.

Systematic Risk

Systematic risk results from conditions, events and trends occurring outside the scope of the investment. At any one point, there are different degrees of each risk occurring. These risks will cause the demand for a particular investment to rise or fall, thus impacting actual returns. The four principle types of systematic risk include the following:

- *Exchange Rate Risk*: The risk that an investment's value will be impacted by changes in the foreign currency market.
- *Interest Rate Risk*: The risk attributed to the loss in market value due to an increase in the general level of interest rates.
- *Market Risk*: The risk attributed to the loss in market value due to the declining movement of the entire market portfolio.
- *Purchasing Power Risk*: The risk attributed to inflation and how it erodes the real value of an investment over time.

Unsystematic Risk

Unlike systematic risk, unsystematic risk is not attributed to external factors. This source of risk is unique to an investment, such as how much debt a company possesses, what actions a company's management takes and what industry it operates in. The principle types of unsystematic risk include the following:

- *Business Risk*: The risk attributed to a company's operations, particularly those involving sales and income.
- *Financial Risk*: The risk attributed to a company's financial stability and structure, namely the company's use of debt to leverage earnings.
- *Industry Risk*: The risk attributed to a group of companies within a particular industry. Investments tend to rise and fall based on what their peers are doing.
- *Liquidity Risk*: The risk that an investment cannot be purchased or sold at a price at or near market prices.
- *Call Risk*: The risk attributed to an event where an investment may be called prior to maturity.
- *Regulation Risk*: The risk that new laws and regulations will negatively impact the market value of an investment.

Summing systematic and unsystematic risk equals total risk. Since the goal of asset allocation is to create a well-diversified portfolio, unsystematic risk is considered unimportant because it should be eliminated with proper diversification. Therefore, an optimal portfolio should only possess systematic risk, or risk resulting from market and other uncontrollable external factors.

Measuring Investment Risk

Since different investments have both different types of risk and different degrees of risk, it is essential to quantify risk in order to make comparisons across the broad range of asset classes. As mentioned earlier, risk can be defined as the uncertainty that actual returns will not match expected returns. Intuitively one can see that the greater the difference between actual and expected returns, the less predictable and uncertain that investment is considered. This translates into greater risk.

Using historical return data, we are able to define risk more accurately. Historical volatility data can be obtained using numerous intervals of time – days, weeks, month and years. Monthly volatility is generally used in practice. In simple analysis, averaging the degrees of difference between actual and expected returns for a given investment gives us the statistical measure called standard deviation. A higher standard deviation means higher risk.

One important note to remember is that standard deviations for investments or asset classes are not static. They will change over time. Some asset classes will change more frequently and to a greater degree than other asset classes. Historically, small cap stocks have exhibited the greatest amount of variability with regard to standard deviation. Large cap stocks follow right behind.

Volatility has been shown to rise during periods of falling prices and moderate during periods of advancing prices. Even with changes to asset class volatility in the short-term, the range of asset class volatility has remained relatively stable over the long-term. That is good for investment planning. Standard deviation is a statistical measure of the degree to which actual returns are spread around the mean actual return. Expressed as a percentage, standard deviation is considered the best measure of risk.

Since actual returns are impacted by both systematic and unsystematic risks, standard deviation is a measure of total risk. As a result, standard deviation gives an investor a way to evaluate both the risk and return element of an individual investment. Although standard deviation is one of the best measures of risk, it is by far not without issues. Depending on the holding periods selected for comparison, standard deviation may vary from analysis to analysis.

Ten Rules of Risk Reduction

Risk, and the endeavor to reduce investment risk, is as old as the financial markets themselves. Regardless of the new technology, the new hot products or the new financial models, successful investing is all about maximizing the inescapable trade-off between risk and return. The following is a list of ten rules you may want to consider for reducing the level of risk in your portfolio.

1. *Understand Your Risk*: Knowing your level of portfolio risk will enable you to make better and more informed decisions.
2. *Build a Multi-Asset-Class Portfolio*: Holding multiple asset classes will smooth the risk volatility you would otherwise experience from holding only one asset class.
3. *Target Low Correlations*: Low correlations further smooth out risk volatility since lower correlations means the less two asset classes move in tandem with each other.
4. *Add Fundamentally Different Asset Classes*: Asset classes that are fundamentally different exhibit return enhance and risk reduction potential. Hold a combination of these asset classes.
5. *Diversify Each Asset Class*: Diversification is not the same as asset allocation. Diversify each asset class to reduce unsystematic risk, or investment-specific risk unique to single investments.
6. *Reoptimize Your Portfolio*: Reoptimization involves rebalancing your allocation mix to optimal targets, reallocating contributions to under-allocated asset classes and relocating assets for maximum tax and income efficiency.
7. *Use Common Sense*: When selecting the suitable level of risk for your portfolio, it is more important to be approximately correct, than to be precisely wrong.
8. *Hedge Risk*: Although not for all investors, hedging risk with options, swaps, futures and position neutralizing short sales can protect against severe market declines.
9. *Exercise Discipline*: Employing a steadfast approach to enhancing your risk-adjusted return will outperform a constantly changing approach.
10. *Consider Assistance*: Risk is best managed by experienced people, not financial models. Professional help may provide you with the resources you need.

Introduction to Asset Allocation

Please do not get confused by the title of this section. This section is not necessarily about allocating the assets in your hedge fund portfolio, but rather how to incorporate hedge funds into a properly allocated portfolio. Asset allocation and hedge fund investing can form a very powerful combination. A properly allocated portfolio will typically include equity investments, fixed-income investments, and alternative investments. This is where hedge funds can play a big part. Since this book is about hedge funds and not asset allocation, the content in this chapter will only touch the surface and be more general in nature.

Asset allocation is best described as dividing your investment portfolio and other investable money into different asset classes. The concept underlying allocating your portfolio in such a way is that by splitting your investment portfolio into different asset classes you will reduce portfolio risk and enhance your long-term risk-adjusted return. In other words, asset allocation provides you with your best opportunity to earn solid returns over time while assuming the level of portfolio risk most suitable for your unique situation. The allocation of your assets is based on a number of very important factors, such as current financial position, investment time horizon, level of wealth, financial goals and obligations, and risk profile. There are a few other variables, or portfolio allocation inputs as I like to call them. Specifically, the three most important inputs that determine your asset allocation are your financial objectives and obligations, your investment time horizon, and your risk profile. For building an optimal portfolio, your unique risk profile is of utmost importance. Your risk profile includes three variables – your tolerance for risk, your capacity for risk, and your need to assume risk.

Empirical research clearly articulates what drives portfolio performance over the long-term, your asset allocation. Let's put that macro viewpoint into a useable set of factors, a micro viewpoint, as follows:

- The asset classes you will employ
- The percentage of your total portfolio that you will allocate to each asset class
- The parameters you set that triggers rebalancing – based on time or deviations
- The investment style you select – active management or index funds and their types
- The level of portfolio diversification
- The application of low correlations
- The tax status of your portfolio – tax-exempt or taxable
- The total tax bracket you are in

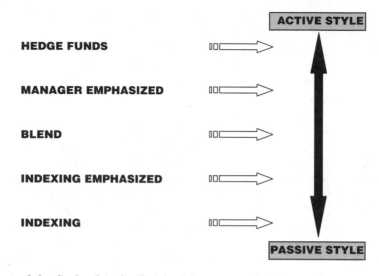

Figure 3-3   Scale of Active-Passive Management Style

Al-Location, Al-Location, Al-Location

One of the leading adages of classic wisdom most synonymous with business success is "location, location, location." Nearly everyone has heard of this phrase because it is so very true. Building a successful business is not very different from building a successful portfolio. This exact same classic wisdom applies to investment success as well, but expressed with a twist – "al-location, al-location, al-location." Location, or al-location in this case, can mean the difference between feast or famine. Moreover, where you locate can mean life or death of a business and the same is true with investing. There are no short cuts and cutting corners will ultimately be an investor's downfall.

Before selecting a location, business owners do their homework; they do not rely on their own perceived superior instinct. They know that doing so will not get the job done. As an investor, you should approach your investing in the same manner. Prudent investors do not make the mistake of thinking that because their previous investment pick worked out, they are geniuses at picking new successful investments. Through experience you will know what constitutes a properly allocated portfolio and thus position yourself for long-term success. A factor whose true importance cannot be underestimated or underappreciated is al-location.

Asset Allocation Analogy

To better help people understand the significant benefits of asset allocation, I often times use a hockey analogy. The analogy goes something
like this. Employing asset allocation is similar to a hockey player wearing
protective equipment – helmet, shoulder pads, kneepads, etc. If that
hockey player were to take off his protective equipment, he could probably skate faster, cut easier and pass the puck better. As a result, he would
probably be a scoring machine. However, it doesn't take a rocket scien-
tist to recognize that not wearing the proper protective equipment is not
at all practical and very unwise and foolish. One hit into the boards from
your opponent and you could be out of the game for a very long time, if
not forever. So why risk it?

Investing and asset allocation are quite the same. An investor who
does not wear his proper protective equipment may experience uncommonly superior returns in the short-term, but will eventually take the
same hit that a hockey player would and therefore badly hurt him or
knock him out of the game completely. Taking a hit may not happen
right away or sometime thereafter, but it will happen at some point. The
question is not if, but when?

Asset Allocations Evolve Over Time

Portfolios and the asset allocation comprising a portfolio will not
remain static over time. At some point in the future your personal situation will change and so too will your asset allocation in response.
There are multiple factors that may change and each plays a role in
determining your optimal asset allocation. Some of these factors called
the portfolio allocation inputs include your risk profile, your current
and future financial position and your investment time horizon. In
addition to your personal situation changing, market factors impacting your portfolio will also change to some degree over time. These
"market-centric" portfolio allocation inputs include expected total
returns for your investments, the volatility risk of investments and the
trading flexibility of those investments you own and/or are targeting
for investment purposes. Rest assured, asset allocation promotes quick
and easy changes to your portfolio, thus you will not need to spend
hour after hour researching what decisions should be made and then to
implement them.

Key Benefits of Asset Allocation

Asset allocation maximizes the risk-adjusted return of a portfolio. In addition, asset allocation also minimizes portfolio volatility risk and provides for a sound investing discipline. Specifically, the key benefits of asset allocation include the following:
    Asset allocation...

- Minimizes Retirement Plan Losses
- Promotes an Optimal Portfolio
- Eliminates What Does Not Work
- Supports Quick and Easy Reoptimization
- Maximizes Portfolio Risk-Adjusted Return
- Promotes Simple Portfolio Design and Construction
- Allows for Easy Contribution Decisions
- Minimizes Portfolio Volatility
- Minimizes Investor Time and Effort
- Promotes a More Diversified Portfolio
- Provides Maximum Avoidance of Market Weakness
- Delivers the Highest Impact Value
- Reduces Trading Costs

Common Portfolio Allocation Methods

Once your objectives and constraints are determined, your next task is to work toward allocating your assets suitable to your objectives. This task involves allocating assets to specific asset classes and asset subclasses that will enable you to build your optimal asset allocation.

    Creating your own asset allocation is much like baking your own pie. You will first decide what the purpose of the pie is – perhaps for Christmas, for New Year or for a birthday. Once you have the purpose established, you will then narrow down what kind of pie you will make. Then you will need to identify what ingredients you will need and how best to bake your pie. Your choices of ingredients can vary widely from apple, pumpkin, lemon or blueberry. Toppings also can be added for extra zing. Once you are finished you have a pie that fits the occasion.

    Determining your asset allocation and building your portfolio utilizes much the same process. The purpose for building your portfolio can vary widely, but most encompass some sort of retirement savings.

Thereafter you will need to select the proper asset classes. There are many methods for accomplishing this task.

The most common methods used by investors and investment professionals include equity overload, simple 110, cash flow matching, risk avoidance, allocation timing, and custom combination. All of these models have their advantages and disadvantages. None is absolutely perfect. A discussion of each method is provided below.

Equity Overload

Not withstanding risk, equity assets have outperformed all other primary asset classes over time. Within equities, small cap stocks have performed better than blue-chip stocks. This is the rationale that many investors and financial professionals use as support for a portfolio with nearly all equity, if not all equity. As long as an investor has a long-term time horizon, overloading to equities can be a way to earn solid portfolio performance over time. Beware, however, since this method does not take risk into account, the volatility can be extraordinary and the risk of substantial loss uncommonly high. Not for the faint at heart.

Simple 110

This is one of the most commonly recognized methods for determining asset allocations. However, I have slightly remodeled it for 110 rather than the traditional 100. Under this model, you allocate to equities based on the equation 110 minus your age. The remaining portion is allocated to fixed-income. For example, a 65 year old investor would allocate 45 percent to equities (110 – 65) and the remaining 55 percent to fixed-income.

The underlying assumption of this model is that the investor will live well into retirement years and that his or her risk tolerance will decline with each passing year. The obvious drawback to this method is that it does not take into account many unique factors, such as risk tolerance, risk capacity, need to assume risk, and level of wealth.

Cash Flow Matching

Cash flow matching attempts to match your anticipated future financial obligations, your cash outflows, with your anticipated cash inflows, both non-investment income and investment income. The first step in this model is to identify all anticipated future financial obligations. The second step is to identify all anticipated future financial inflows from non-investment sources. Some sources of non-investment income include wages, social security and inheritance. Once these two steps have been accomplished, you will then determine the gap between the two. The fourth step is to evaluate your current portfolio against what will be needed from your portfolio in the future to fill the gaps in cash flows. This evaluation will determine what performance you will need to achieve whether that means growth or preservation. For example, an investor determines that he will need to earn 10 percent per year in his portfolio for his retirement. Since corporate bonds have historically earned less than 10 percent annually and while equities have historically earned greater than 10 percent annually, the investor will need to allocate some to equities and some to corporate bonds. Other combinations of high-yield bonds, small cap stocks, international equities and real estate investment trusts can be included as well.

The key is to match anticipated cash outflows with anticipated cash inflows and identify if your portfolio is large enough to fill the gap. If the gap between what you will need and what your non-investment sources can provide is small, a small conservative portfolio may be appropriate. Although an investor may have the tolerance and capacity to assume risk, he or she may not have the need to assume additional risk, especially useless risk that will provide no benefit.

Forecasting skill, life expectancy and uncontrollable market factors are some of the drawbacks of employing this asset allocation method.

Risk Avoidance

Regardless of risk capacity and return need, some investors simply do not want to take risk. They can't stomach it. As a result, allocating to conservative assets may be the most appropriate thing to do. Although investors in this situation may not be in the best position to accomplish their goals and objectives, they surely will sleep better at night. This gets at the root of behavioral finance and investing.

Allocation Timing

Under this model, an investor or portfolio manager will change asset allocations in the hope of capturing short-term profits on asset classes showing the most strength. This is obviously a timing strategy that numerous studies have shown to be fraught with error and concluded to rarely work. The allocation timing method involves allocating to asset classes when they are out of favor, such as equities during bearish stock markets; with the hope of selling at the peak of when they are in favor, such as bullish stock markets. Information, care and skill for making such calls are absolutely critical for success.

Custom Combination

Since many of the methods discussed have one or more drawbacks to them, developing a custom combination may therefore prove quite beneficial. Many financial professionals have gone this route and designed their own unique method that utilizes the best from one or more of the methods. The vast majority employs some sort of cash flow matching combined allocation timing method. Doing so allows them to establish an asset allocation best suitable for their investor while allowing them to promote their care and skill in portfolio management. Using a custom combination may be a smart move for you, depending on your situation. Many financial advisory firms offer their own unique method to ensure you do your due diligence before signing on.

In the next chapter, you will learn about the fundamental differences between the two most popular and well-known actively managed and pooled investment vehicles, mutual funds and hedge funds.

4

Battle for Portfolio Performance: Hedge Funds vs. Mutual Funds

Just about every investor has heard about mutual funds and most understand how they work conceptually. Hedge funds are similar, at least conceptually. That is where the similarities end as mutual funds and hedge funds differ in many ways. The primary differences include degree of regulatory oversight, investment strategies available and employed by the managers, degree of liquidity, fees charged, and types of investor each is permitted to accept. This chapter will discuss in detail each of these primary differences as well as some of the secondary and less important differences.

Sports Cars and Minivans

The investing marketplace is comprised of many different traditional and alternative methods of investing, with the pooling of funds being one of the most popular. Two of the most popular vehicles of pooled funds are hedge funds and mutual funds. But how are the two different in basic terms?

A good way to think about the difference between hedge funds and mutual funds is to consider the difference between a sports car and a minivan. If mutual funds resemble minivans then hedge funds resemble sports cars. Both minivans and sports cars are conceptually the same – to transport one or more people from location A to location B. But, as we all know, minivans and sports cars are classic examples of how two things differ. This is the beginning of the great divide between mutual funds and hedge funds. Going back to our analogy, sports cars are faster off the line, have higher top speeds, are more nimble, significantly more maneuverable, and can go where many other vehicles dare not venture. At the same time, however, sports cars are limited in the number of passengers they can carry, attract the attention of the police to a higher degree, require a more polished driver, and have substantially lower safety features if it were to get into a crash. The same positives and negatives can be said of hedge funds and mutual funds. By far the greatest drawback to hedge funds is the potentially higher risk involved, as it can be with sports cars. This risk can be controlled by the driver, or manager as is the case with hedge funds.

Let's continue our analogy to compare and contrast hedge fund risk. First, it is not a forgone conclusion that investing in hedge funds is any riskier than mutual funds. As with driving a sports car and minivan, the driver and the actions he or she takes is what dictates risk. Driving fast, darting in and out of traffic or going through red lights can be done by drivers of either sports cars or minivans. However, one can argue that different types of drivers select different type of vehicles. More conservative drivers will typically not drive, let alone buy, a sports car. Thus, hedge funds probably attract managers who prefer the higher risk and are comfortable with taking heightened risk. Furthermore, regardless of the type of driver who is behind the wheel of a sports car, at some point that driver is going to open things up and see what they've got. The same can be said for hedge fund managers. Regardless of the risk profile, hedge fund managers may feel compelled at some point to take a somewhat riskier position.

The final point to this analogy is how each protects passengers in the case of an accident. Regardless of the vehicle, passengers are at greater risk traveling on expressways and major streets. Side streets and subdivision streets are typically not a significant risk. In this analogy, streets represent specific segments of the market. For example, micro-cap and small-cap equity stocks are the expressways, while money markets and short-term fixed-income products are subdivision streets. Getting into an accident on the expressway at 70 miles per hour will be devastating regardless of whether or not you are driving a sports car or minivan. The important point here is that the type of investments held in the fund will determine a majority of the overall risk. Thus, the skill and talent of the manager is very important.

Primary Differences

The following discussion will compare and contrast mutual funds with hedge funds. Mutual funds are best described as traditional investments while hedge funds are best described as alternative investments.

Regulatory Oversight

Mutual Funds

Mutual funds must register with the Securities and Exchange Commission (SEC) as investment companies and in doing so they are subject to strict regulation. Mutual funds are specifically regulated by four federal laws. These laws include the Securities Act of 1933, the Securities Act of 1934, the Investment Company Act of 1940, and the Investment Advisers Act. Other governmental and industry associations also play a role in regulating mutual funds. In addition to the SEC, the Internal Revenue Service and the National Association of Securities Dealers, or NASD, provides oversight to some degree. The IRS provides oversight regarding a fund's portfolio diversification and its distribution of earnings. The NASD on the other hand focuses its resources on mutual fund advertisements and related sales materials. Lastly, regulations specify that 75 percent of each mutual fund's board of directors must be independent of the fund's management team.

Some of the requirements imposed on mutual funds and policed by the appropriate associations include keeping detailed books and records, providing daily liquidity, valuing shares accurately and on a daily basis, and restrictions on the level of risk mutual funds can assume. Additionally, all mutual fund shareholders must be given a prospectus prior to investing.

Hedge Funds

Hedge funds are not subject to the same regulations as mutual funds since they are not required to register with the SEC. In 2004, the SEC began to require all hedge fund managers to register. However, in the summer of 2006 this requirement was struck down by the courts of the United States. New methods to require managers to register will surface as this is a top priority of the SEC.

Hedge funds are required to provide certain materials to prospective investors. These materials include an offering memorandum, limited partnership agreement (or something similar) and a subscription agreement. Each document will provide some degree of disclosure about the hedge fund.

Due to the lack of oversight, hedge funds are given substantially more freedom in managing their hedge funds using a variety of strategies. Some of these strategies are conservative and some aggressive, with most somewhere in between.

From an investor's perspective, mutual funds are more ideal since the activities of managers are policed and regulated by the SEC. This provides comfort to the investor in knowing that all is well with the management and security of their investment.

Investment Strategies

Mutual Funds

Mutual funds are very limited in the strategies they can employ to manage money. Practically the only investment strategy mutual fund managers can employ is traditional buy and hold. Managers cannot sell short, nor leverage their funds. At the same time, managers are somewhat handcuffed on the type of investments they can hold. Non-investment grade securities are for the most part off limits and so too is any form of market timing. Suffice it to say that mutual fund managers drive a minivan that can only go forward. They cannot go in reverse.

Hedge Funds

Hedge funds come loaded with available investment strategies. Managers can sell short, implement arbitrage, employ leverage, or even use derivatives for any number of purposes. This gives the hedge fund manager a sizeable advantage over mutual fund managers. Over time, this advantage has translated into better returns and with lower volatility than mutual funds. No wonder why so many mutual fund companies are starting their own hedge funds.

Hedge funds clearly dominate mutual funds given the investment strategies available for the managers to employ. As a result, this is ideal for investors as it increases the probability of generating attractive performance. This performance could be the protection of principle or the growth of capital.

Liquidity

Mutual Funds

This factor heavily favors mutual funds over hedge funds, but that is the nature of the investment vehicle and the inherent trade-off. Without a doubt, mutual funds offer the best liquidity. Investors can call his or her mutual fund, place a sell order and receive a check for the proceeds within a week or less. This is attributed to the type of investments that mutual funds hold. These investments are securities traded on exchanges that exhibit highly liquid markets where buy and sell orders can be placed and executed quickly.

Providing substantial liquidity is a high priority of the SEC. As long as a manager wants to deal with the general investing public, that manager must offer daily liquidity. However, to market to the general investing public the SEC imposes restrictions on the type of investment strategies mutual fund managers can initiate. This is the trade-off mutual funds choose to make. As a result, the aim of mutual funds cannot be on generating the highest performance possible given the restrictions on what they can do, but rather their aim is on generating assets inflows from investors. This is evidenced by their desire to market to the general investing public.

Hedge Funds

Hedge funds provide minimal liquidity, but there is good reason behind this fact. In order for hedge funds to plan, implement, and run their investment strategies, extra time is commonly needed to see the benefits. This is even more important when the investments in the hedge fund are somewhat illiquid themselves. Therefore, hedge fund managers need time to evaluate how best to sell the asset and at a fair price. This time period causes liquidity issues. Hedge funds address this situation by placing restrictions on when investors can withdraw their investments. This is called the lock-up period. Most hedge funds only allow for quarterly, semi-annual, or annual withdrawals. By not providing daily liquidity, hedge funds are restricted by the SEC on the types of investors they can accept. Hedge funds cannot accept investors deemed to be a part of the general investing public. However, hedge funds can accept high-net worth investors who meet certain thresholds. Thus, hedge funds forgo the freedom of marketing their funds.

One significant benefit hedge funds gain by not providing daily liquidity is that that are not handcuffed by the type of investment strategies they can employ. That is the trade-off hedge funds are willing and able to make.

Mutual funds provide daily liquidity while hedge funds do not. All else being equal, more liquidity is better. However, there is a trade-off with offering greater liquidity and that is restrictions on the investment strategies available to mutual fund managers. This in turn sets the scene for a more challenging attempt to generate attractive performance.

Fees

Mutual Funds

The fees mutual funds charge their investors come in two forms. These two forms include an annual management fee based on the amount of assets managed and a sales commission paid when buying and selling the mutual fund. Many mutual funds do charge this sales commission, or load, but many more do not. Given the number of mutual funds available in the marketplace, do not be coerced into buying a mutual fund with a sales commission. Avoid it whenever and wherever possible. As for the annual management fee, this fee is deducted daily but prorated as if it were an annual fee.

The typical equity mutual fund charges a fee of 1.25 to 1.50 percent of assets managed. Be advised, however, that the performance of most mutual funds cannot best the performance of the overall market. Every year there are mutual funds that beat the market, but that is simply the laws of large numbers. Exchange-traded funds offer the potential for attractive performance with low costs.

Hedge Funds

The typical hedge fund will charge two types of fees. The first is an annual management fee quite similar to that charged by mutual funds. The second fee is unique to hedge funds and that is the performance incentive fee. This fee is typically 20 percent of the investment profits and deducted annually. Thus, if a hedge fund generates a $100,000 profit, then $20,000 would be charged to the investor as the fee. Certain safeguards, such as hurdle rates and high-water marks are available to protect investors from performance issues. These issues include low returns that could be generated by another investment without fees and paying fees on profits that were generated previously, but subsequently lost. Only hedge funds can charge the performance incentive fee. Mutual funds are not permitted to charge this fee unless they also partake in the losses of their clients.

Who wants to pay any more than they have to? Since hedge funds charge performance incentive fees, the advantage goes to mutual funds. However, remember that performance incentive fees are only charged on profits generated, thus the net return is what matters most. A fee of 20 percent for a high return can still net more than 0 percent of a low return. Hedge funds are better positioned to generate positive attractive returns, while the same cannot be said for mutual funds.

Types of Investors Permitted

Mutual Funds

Mutual funds are allowed to invest money for nearly all investors regardless of their net worth. They are permitted to do so as a result of the SEC subjecting them to stringent investment and operational requirements. Mutual funds are surely the investments for the general investing public.

Hedge Funds

Hedge funds are severely restricted by the number and the types of investors they are allowed to accept. This restriction is placed on hedge funds by the SEC as a trade-off for the freedom of employing nearly any investment strategy desired. The SEC only permits hedge funds to accept investors that fit the definition of "accredited investor." To quality for this definition, investors must pass some basic net worth hurdles, such as having earned at least $200,000 annually in income for the past two years – and have a reasonable expectation of doing so into the future – and having a net worth of at least $1,000,000 after excluding personal residences and automobiles. In addition, hedge funds are limited to a low number of investors. Thus, hedge funds are relatively constrained in the amount of assets they can manage. This is a benefit to investors as it provides greater access to managers and thus more accountability with performance. One method investors can use to bypass this SEC restriction is to invest in funds of hedge funds. Funds of hedge funds are considered one investor and thus avoid the restriction on the number of investors permitted.

For investors that qualify, hedge funds may be the better route to invest. For the general investing public, mutual funds may be the best, and perhaps only, option.

Secondary Differences

Now that we have discussed the primary differences between mutual funds and hedge funds, we turn our attention to the secondary differences. These differences can be quite large, but are not as important to the decision to invest in mutual funds or hedge funds as are the primary differences.

Valuation and Pricing

Mutual Funds

Mutual funds are required to value their funds and provide prices on a daily basis. This is done once per day after the close of trading. Mutual fund shares are purchased and sold at the single price that is determined for each mutual fund. This practice is essential for providing liquidity to investors. Without a daily price, investors cannot buy or sell their shares. Mutual fund companies place a significant emphasis on generating prices accurately and quickly. Early in my career, I worked in the mutual fund accounting department at Stein Roe Mutual Funds in Chicago. One thing is for sure, the department became a hurried place after the close of the market. It definitely was a rewarding and exciting experience, however.

Hedge Funds

Hedge funds do not provide daily pricing. Moreover, the vast majority of hedge funds do not provide weekly or even monthly prices. Prices, or valuations, are calculated for the time when investment withdrawals and contributions are made. Investors are not necessarily impacted since they will still receive periodic reports showing the total value of their investments. By not providing more timely pricing, this is both good and bad for investors. This practice is bad since investors may not know where they stand at any given point between periods of valuation. However, by not providing frequent valuation reports, hedge fund managers will be lifted from this burden and can instead focus their time and resources on managing the fund.

Culture and Organization

Mutual Funds

Most mutual funds are gigantic organizations. They employ numerous managers, vast numbers of research analysts and even greater numbers of support staff. This creates a more cumbersome cultural style than hedge funds. As a result, mutual funds move much less quickly than do hedge funds. Mutual funds will typically meet to discuss certain investments before making a purchase. The same is not true with hedge funds. Because of this cumbersome culture, mutual funds are presented as minivans in the aforementioned comparison of mutual funds to hedge funds.

Hedge Funds

Hedge funds on the other hand are typically much smaller organizations with a flat organizational structure. Typically, most hedge funds are run by one or two key people. This means that hedge funds can quickly and easily take investment action (e.g. place buy or sell trades). Most hedge funds manage much lower assets under management, thus they are more nimble than mutual funds. This smaller organizational structure is permeated throughout the company. Access to managers is much easier to obtain with hedge funds than with mutual funds.

Performance Objective

Mutual Funds

The primary performance aim of mutual funds is to outperform other mutual funds and traditional managers in their peer group. With mutual funds, the aim is to generate attractive relative performance. Relative to others that is. No objective is established to generate a certain level of return, such as at least 1 percent or better than 10 percent. This means that mutual fund managers approach their investing decisions in a much different way than do hedge fund managers. Mutual fund managers are happy with a return of –5 percent if their peers generated a return of –7 percent. The same is not true of hedge fund managers.

Hedge Funds

The single performance aim of nearly all hedge funds is to generate an attractive absolute return. Said another way, hedge funds strive to deliver returns that are not only positive, but also attractive. Although hedge funds will want to best their peers in performance since investors are attracted to this aspect, most hedge funds will not establish a goal of doing so.

Delivering absolute returns is a defining characteristic of hedge funds. Given the restriction on selling short, mutual funds are handcuffed and greatly limited in their ability to deliver absolute returns. Thus, they do not have a stated goal of such. Hedge funds, given their ability to sell short, can deliver positive returns in any market – up, down, or sideways. Consequently, achieving their goal of delivering attractive absolute returns is not out of reach. The top managers will demonstrate consistency in doing so. Lastly, given the two different performance aims, mutual funds and hedge funds differ in the way they are measured by others. Mutual funds are primarily measured only on relative performance while hedge funds are primarily measured on absolute performance. This provides investors with options, and that is always better.

Volatility

Mutual Funds

The degree of volatility all depends on how the market is performing and in what market or sectors a mutual fund is investing. For instance, a small cap equity fund is much more volatile than a mutual fund investing in large-cap equity securities. Furthermore, a large-cap equity mutual fund will be more volatile than a balanced mutual fund that invests in both equities and fixed-income assets.

Hedge Funds

Hedge funds can be quite the same as mutual funds as the volatility depends on the type of investments held in the fund and how well the market is performing. However, hedge funds are typically less volatile than mutual funds because many hedge fund managers will sell short some of the assets. Thus, regardless of the direction of the market, the assets in the hedge fund will be shielded to some degree from the swings. Given hedge fund managers' ability to sell short, most hedge funds are less volatile than mutual funds. This means that, all else being equal, hedge fund portfolios will be less risky than mutual fund portfolios. A clear advantage for hedge funds.

Source of Risk

Mutual Funds

Traditional investments, including mutual funds, are exposed to three sources of risk. These include risk relating to the market, risk relating to the investment strategy employed to manage a portfolio, and risk associated with how well or how poorly that investment strategy is employed.

By far, the greatest risk associated with traditional investing is the investment strategy used. The second most important is market risk. Be advised that some investment professionals and financial authors will tell you that the greatest risk is market risk. That is not the case at all. If you simply invest in one type of asset or asset class, then perhaps that claim is correct. But investors typically do not do such a ridiculous thing. For instance, if you only invested in real estate and had no stock or bond holdings, then your primary risk would come from how well the real estate market performed. The same can be said for bond investors. If you only invest in municipal bonds, then the primary risk would come from prevailing market interest rates. If rates were rising then your portfolio would take a hit, while if rates were falling then your portfolio would gain. However, if you employed an investment strategy of proper asset allocation, then you would not be subject to the full weight of one market. At times, one asset class will be performing well while at other times other asset classes will be performing poorly. A properly allocated portfolio will protect you from this scenario. Don't be fooled by the claim that market risk is the primary determinant of risk and return. Once you remove market risk from the equation, the remaining risks are the investment strategy employed and how well the strategy is executed. Studies have demonstrated that the risk from the type of investment strategy employed is the leading risk.

Hedge Funds

Hedge funds are exposed to the same risks as mutual funds. However, given the ability of hedge fund managers to sell short, the direction or performance of the market or markets is a non-issue, or at least it should be. Good hedge fund managers know to diversify this risk away in their fund. In consequence, the two remaining types of risk facing hedge fund investors include investment strategy and skill in employing the investment strategy. What does this mean for investors? This means that

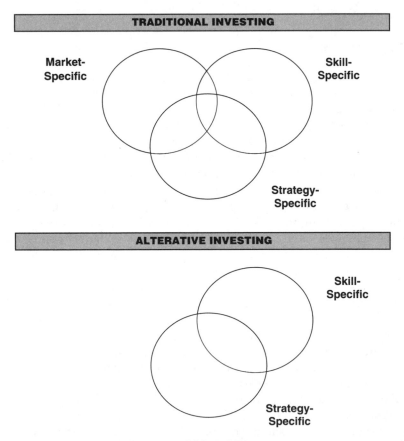

Figure 4-1   Sources of Investment Risk and Return

investors need to exercise extra caution in selecting the right hedge fund manager. Since the performance of the fund is greatly controlled by the actions of the manager, the situation calls for greater scrutiny by investors.

Marketing Practices

Mutual Funds

Since mutual funds are highly regulated by the SEC, the SEC in turn provides mutual funds with more freedom to market their product as they are more comfortable in knowing that the general investing public is protected. Mutual funds are marketing machines with the goal of driving assets into their funds. The more assets they gather, the more money they make and the more money they make proportionately. Since most mutual fund costs are fixed, more assets gained equates to higher margins and greater profitability. This may be important for mutual funds, but this provides no benefit to the common investor. Investors would appreciate mutual funds making more money if that meant more resources would be used to manage their investments thus leading to greater performance. Unfortunately this is not the case.

Hedge Funds

Hedge funds are greatly restricted on how they can market their funds. Since the SEC is less comfortable with the general public investing money with hedge funds, the SEC places hurdles on what type of investors hedge funds can manage money for and how they can market to them. Hedge funds are restricted from placing print advertisements in magazines and from airing commercials on television or the radio. Why? Because the SEC believes that this form of marketing will attract the interest of investors who should not be investing in hedge funds. As a result, hedge funds can only market to people that they believe are screened and satisfy hurdles for high net worth. This can be seen as a negative for investors since investors will not have the best and most complete information to make informed decisions. This could cause some investors to miss appropriate hedge fund managers and instead select a less appropriate and desirable investment fund and investment manager. A clear disadvantage to investors.

Business Relationship

Mutual Funds

Investors to mutual funds are simply that, just investors. These investors do not have a vested interest in the mutual fund as they can withdraw their investment at a moments notice and move to another investment. Mutual funds recognize this and approach investors as if they are just numbers, with dollars signs attached to each fund application.

Hedge Funds

The relationship hedge fund managers and investors have is quite different from that of mutual funds. With hedge funds, the managers, other key decision makers, and investors are, for all intensive purposes, investing partners. Each has a legal interest in the company. This company is typically a limited partnership or limited liability corporation. As a result, investors and hedge fund managers have a strong relationship with aligned interests. Their goal is the same, to see the hedge fund achieve its goal. Hedge fund managers and investors typically work together to see this happen. Investors are not just numbers with hedge funds; they play an integral role in the success of hedge funds.

Tax Considerations

Mutual Funds

Investors in mutual funds and hedge funds are faced with the same types of taxes, capital gains, and ordinary income. However, mutual funds and hedge funds differ in the way investors are exposed to taxable events. With mutual funds, investors will experience ordinary income if the mutual fund distributes dividends and interest income received from the investments the fund owns. That ordinary income is passed to investors who then must report it on their tax returns as investment income. Mutual fund investors can also incur capital gains when they sell their investments. In addition, investors can also receive capital gains distributions when funds distribute capital gains incurred when the funds themselves sell investments they hold. Regardless of whether or not investors sell their shares, they can still incur capital gains taxes simply by funds passing capital gains incurred to investors. Of course, if investors sell their shares for more than they purchased them for, then that will trigger capital gains as well.

CATEGORY	MUTUAL FUND	HEDGE FUND
Liquidity	Daily Liquidity and Redemption	Liquidity Varies from Monthly to Annually
Performance Objective	Attractive Relative Return	Attractive Absolute Return
Regulation	SEC Regulated Investments	Non-Regulated Private Investments
Investors	Unlimited	Highly Limited
Minimum Initial Investment	Typically Very Small, > $1,000	Typically Very High, > $1 Million
Availability	Open to All Investors	Open ONLY to Investors where net worth exceeds $1 million or individual income must have been in excess of $200,000, or joint income must have been in excess of $300,000 in the past two years. Plus investor must expect the same level of income in the subsequent year
Selling Short	Maximum of 30 percent of profits from selling short	Unlimited Freedom to Sell Short
Performance Incentive Fee	Typically No Performance Incentive Fee	Performance Incentive Fee of 20 Percent is Common
Investment Management Fee	Common Usage of 1-2 Percent	Common Usage of 1-2 Percent
Leverage	Practically No Use	Freedom to Use Extensively
Primary Sources of Risk and Return	Market, Strategy, and Skill	Strategy and Skill
Structure	Typically a Large Company	Typically a Small Company
Marketing and Promotions	Unlimited with Disclosure Requirements	Restricted to Only Accredited Investors
Offerings	Prospectus	Private Placement Memorandum
Manager Participation	Little to No Manager Participation	Substantial Capital from Manager Invested
Derivatives	Restricted from Trading	Free to Trade

Figure 4-2   Differences Between Mutual Funds and Hedge Funds

Hedge Funds

Investors in hedge funds typically also incur the same taxes – capital gains and ordinary income. However, hedge funds do not typically distribute these gains or income received to their investors like mutual funds do. By law, mutual funds must distribute at least 95 percent of gains or income received or funds will be subject to taxes themselves.

This provision is not the same for hedge funds. As a result, hedge funds do not distribute their gains and income and instead reinvest them into the fund.

The primary difference with hedge funds is in how they report gains and losses. With hedge funds, gains and losses are reported as a partnership gain on a K-1 form. K-1 forms do not report gains and losses as investment income, but rather as business gains and losses. This is attributed to the partnership organization so many hedge funds typically utilize. In addition, many K-1s are not sent to investors until late in the tax season. This will force investors to delay submitting their tax returns, especially if they like to file early in the tax season.

In the next chapter, you will learn about the tactics and techniques hedge fund managers use to carryout their desired alternative investment strategies.

PART TWO

TOOLS OF THE TRADE AND HEDGE FUND STYLES

5

Tactics and Techniques: Common Practices of Hedge Fund Managers

Hedge fund managers operate under a two-tier system framework. This two-tier system is comprised of the tools and methods hedge fund managers employ and the strategies they commonly use within the context of the tool and methods available. For example, one of the most popular tools employed by hedge fund managers is the use of leverage. However, managers can employ leverage in a number of different ways with the goal of achieving a certain result. This is where the select strategies of the managers come into play. This chapter is specifically dedicated to those tools of the trade that hedge fund managers typically employ to carry out their desired strategy. The remaining chapters in this part dissect the individual strategies that are commonly used.

A good analogy to describe the difference between hedge fund tools and strategies is to consider how food is prepared. Take for example a breakfast plate of eggs. Your strategy is to create a delicious plate of eggs, but how do you prepare them. Do you scramble them, cook them sunny-side up, or perhaps make them into an omelet? This decision represents the tools you have at your disposal. Depending on your skill and available resources, one such idea may be more ideal for you.

The goal of hedge fund managers is to generate an attractive absolute return. In addition, hedge funds aim to generate a rate of return that has a low correlation with the equity markets and from traditional investment managers. To accomplish this, hedge fund managers greatly emphasize the alternative investment strategies discussed in this chapter. Note, however, that many hedge fund managers do not use all of the tools of the trade and that some mutual fund managers even use some of the alternative tools from time to time. The following are the common practices used by hedge fund managers to carry out their desired hedge fund strategy:

- Short selling
- Leverage
- Hedging
- Arbitrage
- Futures and options
- Specific markets
- Position limits
- Buy and sell targets
- Stop-loss restrictions

Common Practices of Hedge Fund Managers

Use of Short Selling

Short selling is selling a security that is not owned by the hedge fund. Many nations around the world restrict this type of technique, but such restrictions are not present in the United States. With short selling, a hedge fund manager borrows shares of a security from a brokerage firm and turns around and sells those shares on the open market. The hedge fund in turn receives the proceeds from the sale, but then owes the shares back to the brokerage firm.

As long as the price of the security declines, then the hedge fund will profit. This follows the tried and true investing wisdom of buy low sell high. However, if the price rises, then the hedge fund will lose as they essentially will have to replace the borrowed shares by purchasing the shares at a higher price. This translates into buying high and selling low. This is not exactly what hedge fund managers should be doing.

In order to borrow shares from a brokerage firm, the hedge fund will need to post some form of collateral, such as other securities. Margin accounts at brokerage firms are therefore required. Margin accounts will contain both the assets used as collateral and the borrowed funds. Hedge fund managers use short selling in one of two primary ways. First, hedge fund managers use short selling as a way of reducing exposure to a single investment. For example, a certain hedge fund holds $25 million in equity securities, comprising 90 percent of the entire fund. Given recent strong price increases, the manager believes the risk and price of equities is too high. To offset some of the risk, the hedge fund manager sells short $5 million, thus reducing open equity exposure to $20 million. Regardless of the price change, either up or down, the remaining $5 million in equities is offset by $5 million in short equities. The second way hedge fund managers use short selling is to profit from perceived overvalued securities. Thus, if a hedge fund manager believes that a certain investment is priced too high, he or she can short sell shares in the hope that the price will fall thus allowing for the hedge fund manager to buy back the borrowed shares and return them to the lender.

Employ Leverage

Leverage is best described as borrowing to buy more of an investment. Furthermore, leverage is assuming more investment exposure than what an investor would be exposed to given the assets that particular investor holds. For example, a hedge fund manager expects the return on a certain investment will experience strong performance over the next year and will deliver a return that exceeds the cost of borrowing funds. As a result, the hedge fund manager invests $2 million in the investment and borrows funds to buy another $1 million in the same investment. Thus, the hedge fund will own an investment worth $3 million dollars and the fund only used $2 million of its own assets.

For another example, take for instance someone who purchases a home for $500,000 where $200,000 is from the homeowner's money and $300,000 is borrowed from the bank. If their home appreciates $100,000 over a certain period than the homeowner will experience a return of 33 percent ($100,000 / $300,000) less borrowing costs. Now suppose the home depreciates even $100,000. That means the homeowner has experienced a return of –50 percent (–$100,000 / $200,000) less borrowing costs. As you can see, the impact of borrowing surely magnifies return. Leverage can also create situations where you can lose more than your original investment. In the previous example, if your home price were to fall $250,000 then you would have $50,000 in negative equity ($250,000 – $200,000 original investment). Hedge funds work the same way. As long as the return is positive, then the return is magnified to the upside. However, when things turn bad, leverage magnifies the bad and can even put the investor in a position where they end up owing money, more than their original investment.

With leveraging, investors and hedge fund managers anticipate a higher return on the borrowed funds in excess of the cost to borrow the funds themselves. Hedge funds borrow these funds from brokerage firms who charge them a rate of interest tied to some standard rate, such as LIBOR. The use of leverage increases risk and therefore should be used cautiously. Leverage magnifies investment performance on the upside and downside. When the market for an investment is performing well, leverage will generate greater returns. However, in falling markets or declines in the price of an investment, leverage can be your worst enemy.

Given the heightened risk with employing leverage, many hedge fund managers have found more low risk ways of using it to their advantage. Two of the most common ways they use leverage are to increase the exposure of a new investment without selling another investment all at one time to provide the funds and to magnify the results of a low-risk, low return strategy, such as price discrepancies and arbitrage opportunities. When used judiciously, leverage can work very well in your favor.

Conduct Hedging

Hedging is used when a manger believes that a certain investment offers profit opportunity, but does not want to be exposed to other risks, such

Strategy	Leverage
Fixed-Income Arbitrage	20 to 30 times capital base
Convertible Arbitrage	2 to 10 times
Merger Arbitrage	2 to 5 times
Equity Market Neutral	1 to 5 times
Long/Short Equity	1 to 2 times
Distressed Securities	1 to 2 times

Source: *"Risk Management for Hedge Funds - A Prime Broker's Perspective"* by *Pascal Lambert and Peter Rose*

Figure 5-1   Degree of Leverage by Strategy

as market risk. For instance, a hedge fund manager believes that a select S&P 500 stock is significantly overpriced. As a result, the hedge fund manager short sells the stock and simultaneously buys an S&P 500 index fund. Thus, the investment is protected from market influences and only price movement attributed to overvaluation is thus experienced. The same can be done for undervalued securities. In this case, a hedge fund manager could buy the security and sell short an S&P 500 index fund. Thus, if the stock declines due to the market in general weakening, then the hedge fund manager will lose money on the long stock position held but offset the loss with the gain from the short S&P 500 index fund held. This tool eliminates and isolates market risk and emphasizes investment-specific risk.

Utilize Futures and Options

Hedge fund managers can utilize options and futures to either speculate or to hedge their positions. For instance, if an equity hedge fund manager believes that the equity market will decline, he or she can protect the value of the hedge fund by either buying S&P 500 put options or selling short S&P 500 futures contracts. Thus, if the market declines the hedge fund manager can exercise the S&P 500 put options to offset the loss with the long equity position or will profit on the decline of the market and given the short futures contract.

Futures and options are both considered derivative products. Many people have biased thoughts about derivatives because of all the media hype surrounding a couple of high profile derivative scandals. Nevertheless, derivatives offer investors and hedge fund managers alike the opportunity to protect their positions in case of adverse price movements or to speculate on the direction of the market.

A futures contract is nothing more than a delayed purchase of a specific investment. In the case of the S&P 500 contract, the futures contract simply states that one party will purchase the S&P 500 from another party who is on the selling side. Again, a futures contract is essentially the same as buying the investment, but only with a fixed delay built in. This type of an investment thus offers symmetrical risk exposure. Options are slightly different, but do accomplish relatively the same thing; that being speculating on the direction of the market or protecting a portfolio from adverse price movements. Options offer asymmetrical risk exposure.

Options give the buyer the right to buy or sell the underlying assets at a predetermined price and at a predetermined point in time. Options do not obligate the buyer to exercise and buy or sell. However, when the option value is in your favor, an investor would be incredibly foolish to not exercise their option as it would equate to throwing money out the window. Futures contracts on the other hand do not give the buyer the right, they obligate the buyer to either buy or sell the investment at a predetermined point in time, but at the value established at that point in time.

Pursue Arbitrage

Arbitrage is defined in the academic world as a riskless investment. Unfortunately this word has been overused and used out of context by those in the investment profession as a way to push their funds. Arbitrage is the simultaneous purchase and sale of two securities that are explicitly tied in some fashion. One of the most popular uses of arbitrage is to profit from differences in the price of a stock and the bond that converts into shares of that stock. For example, Mega Stores stock is selling for $50 a share and its convertible bond is selling for $1030. If the convertible bond allows for converting into 20 shares of stock, then the value an investor would receive from doing so is $1000 (20 shares multiplied by $50). However, with the bond selling for $1030, the investor would be foolish to convert the bond for stock with less value. To profit on this price discrepancy, a hedge fund manager would short sell the convertible bond and buy the stock with the proceeds. The hedge fund would make $30 on each transaction ($1030 – $1000). The hedge fund manager would continue to place this transaction until the price of the convertible bond and stock become closer and the spread narrows.

Target Specific Markets

Hedge funds will often target specific markets, sectors, and asset classes. This is done to give the fund focus and to take advantage of perceived opportunities specific in that market. Hedge funds will often differentiate between geographic locations, such as European and Asian markets, and asset type, such as equities and fixed-income. By targeting specific markets, hedge funds can gain exposure to opportunities not necessarily available in the overall market. For instance, although many U.S. based companies have operations in Europe and profit from gains made there, a hedge fund may desire more exposure to European markets than simply buying U.S. companies with European operations. This can also be ideal for investors since modern portfolio theory says that investing in additional markets or asset classes can enhance return and reduce risk.

Incorporate Position Limits

To safeguard a hedge fund from the loss on any one investment, hedge funds can institute position limits that restrict the size of an investment in any single company to a certain percentage. In addition, position limits can also trigger hedge funds to liquidate certain holdings once losses become too large. For example, a hedge fund institutes a 20 percent limit on how much any one holding may comprise the hedge funds holdings. Regardless of how well the asset is performing, no new investments can be made in the asset above the 20 percent limit. This protects the hedge fund from large swings in value if the price of the asset begins to turn in the other direction.

Set Buy/Sell Targets

In simplistic terms, a buy/sell target is the point at which a hedge fund manager will either sell a held asset given that it is fairly valued or buy an asset because it is perceived as being undervalued. Hedge fund managers will frequently place target prices on securities and when the investment hits one of those price targets, it triggers a buy or sell transaction.

Follow Stop-Loss Restrictions

Regardless of the estimated value of a certain investment, hedge funds are very conscious of the losses they suffer. Client-investors do not appreciate losses very well. In consequence, hedge funds are motivated to sell losing investments once a certain investment reaches a predetermined level of losses. This predetermined point is the hedge fund manager's maximum loss he or she is willing to incur on any one particular investment. Hopefully a hedge fund will not need to implement a stop-loss provision, but they can protect the fund from additional downside pressure.

In the next chapter, you will learn about tactical hedge fund strategies. These strategies aim to profit from making correct bets on which direction the price of an investment will move.

CHAPTER

6

Tactical Hedge Funds: Going for the Gold with Directional Price Strategies

Tactical styles are very popular with hedge fund managers. In fact, more than half of all hedge fund assets are invested using tactical strategies. Of this style, the macro-centric strategy is by far the most used as it is the broadest category at the same time. Many people in the hedge fund trade refer to this style in one of two ways, using either tactical or directional. Both are used interchangeably and mean the same thing.

Many people think of hedge funds and envision managers selling short or leveraging their funds. Although this is commonly performed, it is by far not the only way hedge fund managers operate their funds. Many hedge fund managers employ little to no leverage and the same goes for selling short as well. Tactical hedge funds operate in this manner. Tactical hedge funds, for the most part, employ no leverage and instead operate as long-term and low turnover investments. At the same time, this low turnover minimizes tax consequences and thus makes

91

tactical hedge funds tax efficient. Since many hedge fund investors are required to lock-up their investment in hedge funds for an extended period of time, emphasizing long-term investing is therefore a smart move by the hedge fund manager. Note that some strategies within the tactical style do provide for more liberal use of leverage and selling short, such as equity hedge funds. As mentioned during the history of hedge funds, Warren Buffet was a big player in hedge funds early in his career. His style of choice was the tactical style.

Macro-Centric

This is a strategy whereby a hedge fund manager invests in securities that capitalize on the broad markets, both domestically and internationally. This is considered a "top-down" approach to hedge fund investing. The objective of a macro-centric strategy is to profit from broad changes in markets that are the result of any number of macroeconomic and governmental factors such as government influence and intervention. Macro-centric hedge funds are almost always broad-based in nature, such as playing FX movements or investing in market indices. Rarely do they invest in a small segment of the overall market, such as buying an oil company to profit from strong earnings. Hedge funds do invest in less broad assets, but generally do so using a slightly different strategy. With macro-centric investing, leverage is commonly employed to magnify the results of the investments.

Many macro-centric hedge funds will select a particular market and will usually invest going long rather than have a short-bias. Managers using equity strategies target individual securities while macro-centric hedge fund managers do not. Only the broad markets and broad themes are considered for investment purposes. As a result, macro-centric hedge fund managers will research and make investment decisions based on specific equity markets, foreign exchange markets, and commodity markets, such as gold, oil, steel, and agricultural products.

The objective of macro-centric managers is to identify current valuation and forecasted price movements. Once this is accomplished, investments or bets are made to take advantage of the anticipated price movements. Again, leverage is sometimes used to enhance results. These actions taken by hedge fund managers can be either systematic or discretionary.

The advantage of macro-centric hedge funds is in their ability to take advantage of discrepancies in the current and forecasted price. In addition, they can achieve this by allocating a good deal of the hedge fund's assets to the investment and to do so quickly. Given the scale of some macro markets, making even sizable investments will not impact the market as it will with some smaller and less liquid markets. Of importance to macro-centric managers are very specific conditions, such as current asset valuation or flow of investment funds into and out of certain asset classes, which are used in making investment decisions. Knowing these conditions and how best to take advantage of them can provide attractive added returns to this type of hedge fund.

The source of returns for macro-centric hedge funds comes from the spread between the intrinsic valuation and the current valuation. The greater the spread, the greater the opportunity. Hedge fund managers employing this strategy seek out these opportunities and quickly take advantage of them. The hope is that when the present macroeconomic or political conditions presently driving the asset price abate, the spread will narrow and the hedge fund will see nice returns. These trends are very important with macro-centric investing.

The great challenge with macro-centric investing is in identifying when the best time is to invest in a certain asset. Hedge fund managers ask themselves if the current trends impacting prices are slowing down, getting better, or are relatively level. If the trend in the macroeconomic or political factor is still declining and getting worse, then the hedge fund manager will delay the investment. However, if they determine that things are getting better, then they will typically make their initial investment.

Macro-centric hedge funds have performed well over the last two decades as their performance has surpassed that of the S&P 500 by a material margin. To make the results even rosier, the volatility of macro-centric hedge funds were lower than that of the S&P 500, most likely the result of investing in multiple markets throughout the globe. This combination of markets, as does the combination of securities, reduces total portfolio volatility while enhancing potential return expectations.

Typical Risk: High to Very High	Risk and Return Profile: Risk Enhancer
Value Proposition: Opportunistic Returns	Directional Bias: Both Net Long and Net Short

Sector Specific

Strategy whereby the hedge fund manager invests in both a long holding of equities together with a short sales of equities or equity market indices. Hedge fund managers will typically invest in sectors they are familiar with and knowledgeable about, thus the name of the strategy. Hedge fund managers are attracted to certain sectors due to the growth prospects. Therefore, betting on the direction of the sector with a long investment will take advantage of growth opportunities. To minimize total market risk, hedge fund managers will sometimes sell short the market index, thus leaving the hedge fund exposed to sector-specific risk only. Of course, with sector-specific risk comes sector-specific return potential. That is what hedge fund managers target by using this strategy.

The typical hedge fund using a sector fund strategy will hold a core position in the sector and an opportunity position, which is essentially a trading position. The core position emphasizes long-term appreciation and is seldom sold to make a quick profit. Buy and hold is the name of the game with the core position. However, short-term trading and quick turnover to generate profits is the focus of the opportunity position. Here a hedge fund manager will buy and sell overvalued securities in the sector by either going long for undervalued securities or going short for overvalued securities. The defining objective of this strategy is to use fundamental research and combine that research with sector expertise in order to generate attractive profits. This research typically emphasizes and filters companies for cash flow and earnings.

The obvious disadvantage to this strategy is the lack of options. If the sector declines, then the hedge fund will decline along with it since hedge funds commonly invest in few sectors. There is little asset allocation with this practice. However, this sometimes can be used to the advantage of the hedge fund manager. Given the selling short technique, hedge fund managers can profit in down times as well. Hedge fund managers who get to know the sector well will gain an advantage over other investors. Knowing what impacts the sector and how to take advantage of that movement is one way knowledgeable hedge fund managers make profits in sector specific.

Prior to taking a position in any market sector, hedge fund managers will assess the growth prospects of the sector. This involves forecasting sector growth rates and then comparing those growth rates to other sectors and the overall market. Hedge fund managers will also seek out sectors that demonstrate an edge in information disclosure whereby a wealth of information is available to help hedge fund managers make sound investment decisions. Lastly, hedge fund managers will gravitate to sectors that provide numerous opportunities to profit. These opportunities can include governmental influences, impact from the weather, consumer buying habits, level and direction of interest rates and so on. The greater the number of factors that can impact a sector, the more ways a hedge fund can profit from making directional price bets.

Typical Risk: High

Value Proposition: Opportunistic Returns

Risk and Return Profile: Risk Enhancer

Directional Bias: Both Net Long and Net Short

Managed Futures

Strategy whereby the hedge fund manager invests in commodities with a momentum focus, hoping to ride the trend to attractive profits. Managed futures are required to register as Commodity Trading Advisors (CTAs) and sometimes as Commodity Pool Operators (CPOs). These types of financial instruments trade on regulated exchanges, although some can trade over-the-counter (OTC) with banks and brokers.

Many hedge fund managers will employ leverage to magnify the performance of the managed futures. There are two types of managed futures managers. The first type is the fundamental managers who rely on their experience, research, and judgment to make investing decisions. The second type of manager is the systematic manager. These managers rely on computer models to forecast and make investment decisions. Neither is really any better. Whatever works the best is the key.

Select hedge fund managers will target quick turnover and quick, but limited, profits. This is frequently done as a safeguard against placing larger trades for longer time where risk increases for experiencing a large loss. Many hedge fund managers using this strategy will do so in a very disciplined fashion. Oftentimes they will liquidate their positions if the trend reverses or fails to materialize as expected. This is called getting stopped out, or experiencing profits or losses prematurely.

Typical Risk: High

Value Proposition: Countercyclical

Risk and Return Profile: Risk Diversifier

Directional Bias: Both Net Long and Net Short

Long/Short Equity

The long/short equity strategy is essentially named for the practice of going long or going short equity securities. This type of hedge fund is the most fundamental of all hedge funds and was established by Alfred Jones himself.

Hedge funds managers will go long securities they believe will increase in value and will go short securities they believe will decline in

Chicago Board of Trade (CBOT)	
U.S. Treasury Bonds	U.S. 10-Year Treasury Notes
U.S. 5-Year Treasury Notes	30-Day Federal Funds
CBOT Mini-Sized Down	Corn
New York Mercantile Exchange (NYMEX)	
Crude Oil	Natural Gas
Heating Oil	Unleaded Gasoline
Gold 100 oz.	
Chicago Mercantile Exchange (CME)	
3-Month Eurodollar	S&P 500 Index
E-Mini S&P 500	E-Mini NASDAQ
E-Mini Russell 2000	Euro FX

Figure 6-1   Most Actively-Traded Futures Contracts

value. These hedge funds focus on reducing total portfolio risk by minimizing overall market exposure. Many managers will even use a two-dimensional bet, which means they go long one particular equity security while going short an entirely different equity security. Thus, when the price of the long position rises and the price of the short position declines, the hedge fund will profit on both positions. This of course could go the other way as well with the hedge fund losing on both fronts if the long position declined in price and the short value increased in price.

The two-dimensional investment is primarily employed to minimize market risk. To accomplish this, a hedge fund manager will go long an equity security and then short an equity index. The net result of any such movement in the market, as expressed by the equity index, will be offset by the equity security. The only exposure therefore is the equity security-specific risk and return potential. For managers looking to maximize their stock selections, the two-dimensional investment is ideal. Again market risk is minimized. Pairings, or offsetting investments with securities in the same sector, are frequently done as well. This will minimize any sector-specific risk originating from the initial investment. Exchange-traded funds and stock index put options are also used to minimize market risk.

Although the net exposure is often long, holding a net short position is not out of the norm. The degree of long or short positions depends on the managers forecast of market prospects. Managers will typically emphasize net long positions when they forecast bull markets and emphasize a decreased net long exposure or even a net short position when they forecast a bear market. Theoretically speaking, hedge funds can generate profits with this strategy in any market, regardless of whether prices are moving up or down. Many hedge fund managers will employ leverage to further enhance performance from a long/short strategy.

Lastly, equity long/short hedge funds will typically not outperform long-only portfolios in markets where prices are rising. However, long-only portfolios do not usually do well in markets where prices are falling. Hedge funds can go long or short and take advantage of either market movement. In aggregate, hedge fund portfolios outperform long-only portfolios over time when both bull and bear cycles are included. In addition, given that hedge funds do not move in value as long-only portfolios do in response to changes in the market, they also have lower volatility. Lower volatility translates into lower risk. The end result is a more attractive risk-adjusted return – higher performance over time combined with lower volatility over time. This is the ideal result.

Typical Risk: Moderate to High	Risk and Return Profile: Risk Enhancer
Value Proposition: Opportunistic Returns	Directional Bias: Both Net Long and Net Short

Emerging Markets

Emerging markets is a strategy whereby a hedge fund manager invests in securities of companies from developing, or emerging, countries. These countries typically have emerging financial markets, thus the name of the strategy. These markets commonly offer solid growth prospects that are generally considered volatile with inflation concerns. Given that some foreign markets do not permit short selling, hedge fund managers are limited in the hedging actions they can employ. Other countries do allow selling short and using leverage. However, given the high transaction costs found in many emerging markets countries, selling short and leveraging are for the most part not used. Perhaps as the countries improve their financial markets this will change and so too will the use of leverage and selling short.

Investing in emerging markets takes a good deal of sophistication and expertise. However, once this knowledge and experience is obtained, hedge fund managers become well positioned to take advantage of opportunistic situations. This is oftentimes the result of price inefficiencies between related markets. These inefficiencies create undervalued assets and they instantly become the target of hedge fund managers. Unfortunately, there are many drawbacks and challenges to investing internationally, particularly in emerging markets. These markets are unpredictable, highly volatile, can restrict the flow of capital into and out of the country, and have precarious governmental situations. Managers often specialize in certain types of markets and certain types of hedge fund instruments to best address these issues. In addition, many emerging markets opportunities lack solid business environments, offer poor accounting practices, and can be riddled with dishonest and fraudulent local companies and investors. Expertise is thus very important.

Most successful emerging markets hedge funds employ superior information and possess superior expertise regarding the select market. Furthermore, they will also use an on-the-ground presence in these markets to foster better cooperation with local contacts. This is all done in the hope of uncovering undervalued or mispriced securities commonly found in emerging markets areas. Without the volatile business climate and lack of suitable information prevalent in these countries, opportunities would simply not exist. Therefore, it is somewhat of a necessary problem to achieve strong results using this strategy.

The best way that hedge fund managers can generate superior returns in emerging markets is to assemble their own information and conduct their own research to identify undervalued assets. Once the financial conditions in the country are addressed and corrected over time, hedge funds will profit by being one of the first investors in the country before restructuring is made. Over the last two decades, emerging hedge fund managers have done well as they outpaced the S&P 500 with relatively the same volatility. As a result, this hedge fund strategy has become quite popular. Lastly, this strategy is beneficial in that it offers one of the lowest correlations to the other hedge fund strategies. Thus, risk can be reduced and return enhanced with an emerging markets strategy.

Typical Risk: High to Very High   Risk and Return Profile: Risk
                                       Enhancer

Value Proposition: Opportunistic   Directional Bias: Net Long
Returns

Market Timing

Market timing is a strategy whereby a hedge fund manager invests in asset classes that are forecasted to perform well in the short-term. No consideration is typically given to positions held for more than the short-term. Rebalancing of the holdings, or asset classes, is commonly done to take advantage of price rotation and price leadership among asset classes. This strategy relies heavily on the skill of the hedge fund manager with regards to the timing of entry and exit points for each investment.

Hedge fund managers will either go long or go short to take advantage of market timing opportunities. Given the breadth of the marketplace, many long and short positions can be held at one point in time. Hedge fund managers will move across the different strategies opportunistically looking for that diamond in the rough. Here the hedge fund manager may invest in commodities, equities, equity indices, bonds, or even foreign currencies. There are little barriers for the hedge fund investments.

This strategy requires the utmost attention of the hedge fund manager since opportunities and price discrepancies can disappear very quickly. Many hedge fund managers will seek out investments exhibiting a good deal of price momentum, either on the upside or the downside. Regardless of the value of a security, the price may simply advance or decline based on irrational investor cash inflows or cash outflows. Hedge fund managers recognize this and will oftentimes capitalize on it to make a profit. Many investors are relatively aware of this type of strategy and how it is employed.

Some hedge fund managers used this strategy with mutual funds by placing purchase and sell orders at or just after the close of the market to take advantage of pricing spreads. This practice, viewed by many as borderline fraudulent, caused quite a stir on Wall Street with regulators with many prominent investment companies named as culprits. As a result, few if any hedge fund managers presently employ this strategy.

Typical Risk: Very High

Value Proposition: Opportunistic Returns

Risk and Return Profile: Return Enhancer

Directional Bias: Both Net Long and Net Short

Short Selling

Short selling is a strategy whereby a hedge fund manager sells short securities with the objective of buying them back in the future at lower prices. This strategy is employed when the hedge fund manager believes the price for a security is overvalued given present earnings or projected future earnings prospects. Thus, the hedge fund manager seeks to profit from a decline in the price of the security.

Investments can be made in individual companies, sectors, asset classes, or the overall market, such as the S&P 500 index. The hedge fund manager must borrow from a brokerage firm the shares of the security he or she wants to sell. These shares are then immediately sold in the open market at prevailing market prices. The hope of the hedge fund manager is to buy back the shares at a later time and return them to the brokerage firm. All at lower prices of course. If the hedge fund manager can accomplish this – selling short at a higher price and replacing the shares with a purchase at a lower price – then the hedge fund will have profited. However, if the price of the security rises, then the hedge fund will lose money as the price continues to rise. This is because at some point in time the hedge fund manager will need to purchase shares to replace the borrowed shares. Thus, if the price to purchase the shares to replace them is higher than the price the borrowed shares were sold short, then the hedge fund will lose the difference in value. To top such a scenario off, the hedge fund must post collateral against the borrowed shares in the transaction. The following are two examples of how a hedge fund manager will gain and lose from a transaction:

SCENARIO 1: Gain

The Frush Hedge Fund sells short 10,000 shares of Mega Company stock at $50 per share. Two months later the price of Mega stock has fallen to a price of $43 per share, not so mega after all. The manager of the Frush Hedge Fund determines that the stock price of Mega Company is reaching a low point and therefore purchases 10,000 shares at $43 per shares. The 10,000 shares thus replace the borrowed 10,000 shares. The Frush Hedge Fund will generate a gross profit of $70,000.

SCENARIO 2: Loss

At the same time as the Frush Hedge Fund is purchasing 10,000 shares of Mega Company stock, the Smith Hedge Fund sells short 5000 shares at $43. Unfortunately, the price of Mega Company stock rises and continues to rise to $53 per share six months later. With solid growth prospects forecasted for Mega Company, the managers of the Smith Hedge Fund decide to get out of their losing investment and do so by purchasing 5000 shares at $53 per share. As a result, the 5000 shares are returned to the brokerage firm but the hedge fund has a gross loss of $50,000 on the investment.

    Under the short selling strategy, hedge fund managers do not have to hold an entire portfolio of short positions. They can simply be short biased. This essentially means that the hedge fund will have some long and some short positions, but the net position will be short, thus the short bias.

What we have just discussed is a "trading" reason for selling short. However, there is another reason why hedge fund managers use selling short strategies exclusively. This reason is to produce monthly income. When a hedge fund manager sells short a security, that transaction produces proceeds equal to the number of shares multiplied by the price per share sold. These proceeds go back to the hedge fund account at a brokerage firm where they earn interest. Thus, the hedge fund manager has artificially created an income stream that simply did not exist before. Interesting huh? Now, if there are dividends or fixed-income dividend payments made on the security, the hedge fund will have to repay the owner of the borrowed shares. This phenomenon is called short interest rebate and some hedge fund managers are very passionate about using it. Not only can you earn profits if the share price declines, but so to can profits be earned when the price of the shares remains unchanged. If they rise, then the hedge fund is out of luck. Theoretically speaking, a portfolio that is net short where the short positions pay little to no dividends or interest payments should outperform a net long portfolio for the single reason that the portfolio will receive a short interest rebate.

Typical Risk: High to Very High	Risk and Return Profile: Risk Diversifier
Value Proposition: Countercyclical	Directional Bias: Net Short

In the next chapter, you will learn about event-driven hedge funds and how they target opportunistic and special situations to generate profits.

Event-Driven Hedge Funds: Strategies that Target Opportunistic Situations

Event-driven hedge funds employ strategies that attempt to capture profits from specific one-time opportunistic situations or events. This style is called event-driven because the opportunities hedge funds target are not dependent on the performance of the overall market, but rather driven by special events. This means that hedge fund managers can profit from employing this strategy in any market condition. If the market is rising or falling, the hedge fund manager will not be impacted. What is important to managers is the level of activity that drives these opportunistic situations. As long as the level of activity is robust, then opportunities will be identified and pursued.

There are four primary strategies under the event-driven style. These include distressed securities, relative value, merger arbitrage, and opportunistic events. Although each is similar, they do differ in important ways. The last strategy mentioned, opportunistic events, is a broader and more general strategy, unlike the other three strategies that are more focused and targeted. Each of these strategies is discussed throughout this chapter.

Distressed Securities

This is a strategy whereby a hedge fund manager invests in the equity or debt of struggling companies at typically steep discounts to the estimated value. This spread between the estimated value and the present market value can be attributed to any number of factors, including the restriction of some institutions from owning non-investment grade securities and the resulting oversale of these securities. Most of the companies that hedge funds target with this strategy are usually in or facing bankruptcy or reorganization.

There are other times where the hedge fund manager will sell short the securities of companies in distress as they expect the share prices to fall with worsening conditions. When negative events impact companies, some holders of debt will attempt to sell their holdings for any number of reasons. Given the turmoil surrounding such an event, there are times of imbalance given that there are many more sellers than buyers. This imbalance is a ripe opportunity to some hedge fund managers. Consequently, managers will take positions in the company, as long as the real value of the security is below that of the current market price of course. Real value is derived from either intrinsic value or from relative value, or the value of similar companies or similar financial instruments of the distressed company that are less impacted and thus provide a bogey for valuation. Current market values below both intrinsic and relative values are signals to hedge fund managers that an opportunity for profit may exist.

Many hedge fund managers operate under the premise that the market does not know how to properly react and value companies in or approaching distress. For those hedge fund managers that acquire specialized knowledge of the distressed securities marketplace, identifying and taking advantage of opportunities is all that much easier to generate attractive returns. Note that the holding period may be longer with investing in distressed securities than with traditional investments or other hedge fund strategies because the companies take longer to turn around their operations.

Many companies that find themselves in serious financial distress will file for bankruptcy protection. As long as the creditors of a particular company have confidence in the future prospects of the company, they will work to resolve a financial solution to get the company back on its feet. This will often include exchanging debt for a combination of new equity and new debt, at lower interest rates, however. These new securities of equity and debt are looked upon favorably by hedge funds and often purchased. The holding period could take many years before material positive returns are experienced, however. Hedge funds using this strategy are always on the look out for companies with solid operations, but with heavy debt loads that impact the financial performance of the company.

Since a distressed securities strategy is more event-driven than not, hedge funds can find opportunities for this type of investing regardless of how well or poorly the market is performing. One can argue, however, the majority of companies in distress occur during times of economic hardship, which can oftentimes be periods of market weakness.

Typical Risk: Low to Moderate   Risk and Return Profile:
                                          Return Enhancer

Value Proposition: Opportunistic   Directional Bias: Both Net
Returns   Long and Net Short

Reasonable Value

Reasonable value is a strategy whereby a hedge fund manager invests in securities that are selling at discounts to their perceived value as a result of being out of favor or being relatively unknown in the investment community. This strategy is similar to the distressed securities strategy but places more emphasis on those securities with lower levels of default risk. As a result, hedge fund managers are presented with greater numbers of opportunities under this strategy. It is therefore important for hedge fund managers to conduct proper due diligence to identify those securities that offer the most promising returns with the least amount of risk. Minimizing default risk through the use of this strategy is done as default risk is perhaps the most significant risk inherent in securities facing troubling times. By minimizing default risk, hedge funds will reduce the greatest threat to fund performance, but they also forgo the return potential as well. That is the trade-off reasonable value hedge fund managers are willing to take.

As with distressed securities, hedge fund managers will commonly purchase a particular security and sell short a comparable security to minimize market risk. This will provide the hedge fund with exposure to company-specific risk and return relatively uninfluenced by the overall market. This strategy is not an especially popular strategy among hedge fund managers, but I present it to give you a cursory understanding.

Typical Risk: Low to Moderate

Value Proposition: Opportunistic
Returns

Risk and Return Profile:
Return Enhancer

Directional Bias: Both Net
Long and Net Short

Merger Arbitrage

Merger arbitrage, or what is also called risk arbitrage, is a strategy whereby a hedge fund manager invests in event-driven scenarios where there are unique opportunities for profit. As the name of the strategy implies, these situations include the following unique situations:

• Acquisitions and corporate takeovers
• Legal reorganizations
• Mergers
• Exchange offers
• Cash tender offers
• Recapitalizations
• Leveraged buyouts (LBOs)
• Proxy contests
• Restructurings

Hedge funds will attempt to generate profits based on changes in price spreads between two securities that have historically consistent spreads, but now have changed due to an event. To take advantage of these opportunities, hedge fund managers will typically exchange securities for cash, securities, or some combination of the two. The most common aim of hedge fund managers using this strategy is to go long the securities of the company being acquired and to go short the securities of the company that is making the acquisition. Regardless of the merger related transaction there is always risk involved that the deal will fall through. Consequently, there is commonly a spread between the current valuation based on the announced deal and the value once the deal is finalized. For instance, company A announces that they will acquire all of the stock of company B for $50 when the share price for company B stock is around $44 a share. Almost immediately – after the trading for the stock reopens on the exchange – the share price for company B will rise sharply. But the price will not rise to $50 immediately due to the risk that the deal will fall through. In reality, the price of company B stock will most likely rise to around $49 per share with a $1 spread built in to protect against the deal not moving forward. This is where hedge funds will usually do their research and due diligence on the deal to determine their expectations of the deal progressing as announced. If a hedge fund manager is comfortable with the deal moving ahead, then they will step in and make an investment to capture the $1 spread. More specifically, a hedge fund manager will go long the stock of company B by purchasing shares at $49 and selling short the shares of company A. Once the deal is finalized, holders of company B stock will receive $50 per share, thus generating $1 profit to the hedge fund in this example.

The success of any merger arbitrage deal is based on the deal going to fruition. Deals that are terminated will typically lose money for hedge funds. That is the important consideration and drawback of this strategy. For instance, in the example above, if a hedge fund had purchased shares of company B and sold short shares of company A and the deal were to fall through, then the share price of company B would decline – perhaps to pre-merger announcement levels of $44 – while the share price for company A would rise. Given the short position with company A stock and long position with company B stock, the hedge fund would take losses on both sides of the investment. That's not exactly what hedge fund managers want to see happen. This outcome is always possible with merger-related deals and thus must be taken into consideration very seriously before any initial investment is made.

The primary advantage of this strategy is that it does not depend on the market. Since merger-related transactions occur in both bull and bear markets, there are good prospects to profit for hedge funds that target these event-driven opportunities. The disadvantage is that hedge funds in this space are entirely dependent on merger-related activity. As long as activity is robust, opportunities will exist. Once activity declines, then opportunities will be scarce to find. That means there will be more hedge fund managers chasing fewer opportunities.

Hedge fund managers that pursue merger-related opportunities tend to be highly specialized in mergers and the process companies go through to make them happen. Furthermore, these hedge fund managers are very good at identifying profitable opportunities and employing strategies for taking advantage of them. Their attempt is to capture the spread between two interrelated securities where the spreads have temporarily become abnormal. As a general rule, the narrower a spread between the company making the acquisition and the company being acquired, the lower risk the market perceives the deal to have. Conversely, deals with wide spreads mean that the market perceives there to be much risk with the deal falling through. Instead of hunting for companies that exhibit opportunities to be acquired, hedge fund managers emphasize conducting thorough research and making prudent investments after deals are announced.

Typical Risk: Low to Moderate

Value Proposition: Opportunistic
Returns

Risk and Return Profile:
Return Enhancer
Directional Bias: Both Net
Long and Net Short

Opportunistic Events

Opportunistic events describes a broad strategy employed by hedge fund managers to invest in securities that are experiencing short-term event-driven opportunities. These opportunities are considered one-time events that offer strong returns. These events have defined beginnings, endings, and time periods in between. They are very definable. Such opportunities include, but are not limited to, the following:

- Initial Public Offerings (IPOs)
- Seasoned stock offerings
- Earnings release surprises
- New business awarded
- Addition or departure of key executives

The list of possible opportunities is extensive. This strategy covers all possible stand-alone events that can present opportunities. To capitalize on these opportunities, hedge fund managers will oftentimes employ multiple and rotating hedge fund strategies. Hedge fund managers will paint themselves into a corner if they commit themselves to using just one particular strategy. They must be flexible and proactive.

The opportunistic events strategy is quite similar to the merger arbitrage strategy, but the two strategies are different in two particular ways. First, merger arbitrage strategies focus on merger-related deals, not on extemporaneous opportunities, as opportunistic events hedge fund managers do. Second, merger arbitrage managers will become involved in opportunities once a deal is announced and typically not beforehand. The same is not especially true of opportunistic events managers. Under this strategy, hedge fund managers are proactive in hunting down companies they believe are in strong positions to develop profitable opportunities. Many hedge fund managers will make initial investments in companies they believe will present opportunities even before these opportunities surface. Many traditional investment managers do the exact same thing, so this strategy is not entirely foreign to many people.

As with the other event-driven strategies, the opportunistic events strategy does not rely on the performance of the overall equity or fixed-income markets. As long as special events present themselves, hedge fund managers employing this strategy will generate returns. The financial instruments most commonly used by managers in this space include the following:

- Debt securities
- Warrants
- Preferred stocks
- Common stocks
- Index put options
- Put options spreads

Not only do hedge fund managers emphasize certain financial instruments to make investments, they also use their specialized knowledge of corporate lifecycles and historical price spreads to generate attractive returns. The foundation for this knowledge is derived from appraisal analysis, occurrence analysis, and duration analysis. As long as the prices move as anticipated, given definable short-term events, then the hedge fund will have accomplished their aim and delivered profits to hedge fund investors.

Typical Risk: Low to Moderate	Risk and Return Profile: Return Enhancer
Value Proposition: Opportunistic Returns	Directional Bias: Both Net Long and Net Short

In the next chapter, you will learn about relative value hedge funds that employ arbitrage strategies and significant leverage to profit from mispricings between two securities.

C H A P T E R

Relative Value Hedge Funds: Arbitrage Strategies for Reducing Portfolio Risk

Hedge fund managers who follow strategies for taking advantage of arbitrage scenarios are thought to be relative value style managers. They typically emphasize only one market and make a point of employing hedging to the most profitable way. Relative value style managers do not corner themselves into a long bias or short bias. They do whatever is needed to capture the arbitrage opportunity. This means that the manager will go long to take advantage of the undervalued side of an opportunity and then go short the other side of the arbitrage opportunity. The aim is for the long side to rise in price and the corresponding short side to decline in price. Under this scenario, a narrowing spread between the long and short will generate positive returns for the hedge fund. Likewise, a widening spread will lose money for the fund unless the hedge fund manager establishes opposite positions from the aforementioned scenario. Of all the different hedge fund styles, relative value is the last bastion of hedge funds using pure hedging practices. Capturing profits independent of market movements is the aim of relative value style managers. The degree of success for the hedge fund is thus entirely dependent upon the hedge fund manager and the decisions he or she makes.

In the hedge fund trade, there are three strategies comprising the relative value style, sometimes referred to as the arbitrage style. The managers in each strategy employ generally the same type of hedging techniques and tactics all with the aim of profiting from arbitrage opportunities. However, these managers focus on different markets, thereby differentiating themselves from the other relative value style managers. The three relative value style strategies include the following:

- Convertible Arbitrage
- Equity Market Neutral
- Fixed-Income Arbitrage

Convertible Arbitrage

Convertible arbitrage is a strategy whereby a hedge fund manager takes advantage of perceived price inequality, a scenario that offers low-risk profitable opportunities. This generally involves a hedge fund manager going long in one security and going short in a related security. The most common financial instruments used include a convertible bond and the underlying security. There is a very good reason for this strategy. Convertible bonds are your typical bonds that pay interest, but they offer one important difference, the option for the bondholder to exchange, or convert, the bond to a predetermined underlying equity security. Convertible bonds are issued with preset conversion ratios, such as 20 to 1 or 15 to 1. This means that the convertible bond essentially has two values. The first is the current market price and the second is the implied value based on the conversion ratio and the market price for the underlying equity security. For example, if a convertible bond with a 20 to 1 conversion ratio is selling for $900 and the underlying equity security is selling for $47, then the implied value for the convertible bond is $940. To arrive at this implied value, simply take the conversion ratio, which represents the number of shares you would get if you converted, and multiply by the price per share of the underlying equity security, the security you would receive when you exchange the convertible bond. Thus, in this example the $940 implied value is the $47 per share price for the underlying equity security multiplied by 20, the number of shares you would receive if converted.

So what does this all mean to you and to hedge fund managers? It means there is an opportunity to profit. To do so, a hedge fund manager would buy the convertible bond for $900 and sell short 20 shares of the underlying security for $940. Thereafter the hedge fund manager would convert the bond to the underlying equity security thus replacing the 20 shares of stock sold short. The manager would receive the difference between the two buy and sell transactions, or $40. This may not seem like a ton of money, but when a hedge fund buys 1000 bonds or more, then we are talking about sizable profits. Furthermore, many hedge funds will employ leverage, or using borrowed funds, to make an even bigger investment. So long as the opportunity exists and the return is greater than the borrowing costs, then the use of leverage will make a positive impact to performance. Furthermore, the proceeds received from the stock sold short will provide a short interest rebate.

Now that we have gone through a detailed example of how convertible arbitrage works, I'll pause enough to say that opportunities of that scale do not exist. Hedge fund managers are always on the lookout for profitable arbitrage opportunities and will therefore capitalize on even the smallest opportunity to generate returns. That means that the spread, or difference, in related prices between the convertible bond and the underlying equity stock would have been arbitraged away much, much sooner. The spread never would have reached that level before gaining the attention of hedge fund managers. Narrow incremental arbitrage spread opportunities is what hedge funds typically have to deal with. Leverage becomes all that more important with narrow spreads. Even a narrow spread can provide material profits when substantial leverage is brought to bear. It is rather common for managers emphasizing convertible arbitrage strategies to employ leverage equating to five times or more of the actual hedge fund capital involved.

One of the advantages of convertible arbitrage lies in the hedge fund manager's ability to uncover and exploit opportunities in any market, bull or bear. Since this strategy only involves the mispricing of two related securities, the hedge fund manager does not have to be cautious about how the market will impact the outcome.

Typical Risk: Low

Value Proposition: Reduced Volatility

Risk and Return Profile: Reduced Risk

Directional Bias: Both Net Long and Net Short

Equity Market Neutral

Under this relative value strategy, a hedge fund manager will purchase an equity security and turn around and sell short a related equity index. Selling short the equity index will offset the systematic, or market, risk inherent in the equity security first purchased. The objective is to capitalize on the perceived growth prospects of the equity issue and to minimize the risk of the market from driving down the price. For instance, a hedge fund manager purchases 1000 shares of an oil company for $50,000 and then sells short $50,000, or an amount that offsets the difference in price movements, in an S&P 500 index fund. If the overall market were to decline, then the long stock of the oil company would decline resulting in a loss, but so too would the short S&P 500 index fund resulting in a gain. The net result will be close to a zero profit or loss, although it depends on the correlation between the two instruments. This has in essence hedged the downside risk from market factors. At the same time, if the market were to advance due to favorable economic results, then the hedge fund would profit from the price increase of the oil company, but lose from the unfavorable price increase against the short S&P 500 index fund. The net result of the market movement will be close to zero. Now, take a scenario where company-specific or industry-specific factors impacted prices. Since these are not total market related, the market will see little impact from these factors. However, the prices for companies in the oil sector and the company specifically involved will experience price movements. The net result to the hedge fund will either be a gain from favorable price movement or a loss from unfavorable price movement. In summary, the manager has insolated the hedge fund from market factors, thus leaving the only open exposure to company-specific and industry-specific factors.

The above example only provided a scenario where the hedge fund manager was bullish on a particular security. The tables can be turned around if the manager feels strongly about the bearish forecast for a particular security. Under these scenarios, a hedge fund manager will sell short the selected security and purchase a stock index, again such as the S&P 500. This will minimize market risk and put the onus on the prospects of the individual security sold short.

This strategy places a good deal of the risk on the security selection skills of the hedge fund manager since the market is more or less hedged. The source of returns under the equity market neutral strategy derives from long positions in securities that outperform the market and from short positions in securities that underperform the market. For managers looking to maximize their bets, leverage is employed to purchase more of the investment and sell short more of the market. The results of the security selection are thus magnified.

As with the convertible arbitrage strategy, equity market neutral strategies do not rely on how well or poorly the overall market is performing. Since the aim of this strategy is to hedge market risk, the net result only depends on how well or poorly the individual investment performs. In times of bullish and bearish markets, hedge fund managers can always identify individual securities they believe are either overvalued or undervalued. No matter which degree of misvaluation they find, the hedge fund manager has the tools to take advantage of the opportunity to generate profits for the hedge fund. Equity market neutral positions also benefit from the short interest rebate, much like convertible arbitrage funds do. Again, this is the benefit where hedge funds receive interest on the proceeds from the sold short investment, an investment they didn't own in the first place.

Two last points of note about this strategy. First, it is not especially easy to perfectly hedge market risk for any one particular security. Hedge fund managers do have statistical models using a number of factors, such as correlation and beta, to help them determine how much of the equity index to purchase or sell short. The amount could be right on, but is typically slightly off, thus leaving the fund open to at least a minute amount of market risk. Moreover, relationships and correlations are not static, they change over time. Thus, the hedge originally created may need to be modified at a later date. Second, since both long positions and short positions each are exposed to market risk, then the hedge fund manager can offset some of these positions to minimize market risk without going long or short for each position held. The combination of the long and short individual securities will provide some natural hedging.

Typical Risk: Low

Risk and Return Profile: Reduced Risk

Value Proposition: Reduced Volatility

Directional Bias: Both Net Long and Net Short

Fixed-Income Arbitrage

Fixed-income arbitrage is a strategy whereby a hedge fund manager purchases an individual fixed-income security and simultaneously sells short a similar fixed-income security. The aim of this action is to capture what is thought to be a short-term mispricing of the spread between the two securities. Two fixed-income securities that have traditionally moved together in price where there is a consistent spread between the prices of the two are sought out when the spread deviates from past norms. Aside from pure pricing spreads, hedge fund managers will pursue opportunities where historically consistent spreads have changed with yield curves, mortgage-backed spreads, credit spreads, and statistical arbitrage.

Hedge fund managers pour over a significant amount of data in hopes of identifying spreads that have abnormally become wider or have narrowed. This presents opportunities for managers to make investments in hopes that the spreads return to historical levels thus driving profits for the hedge fund. Let's look at an example of this strategy used in practice. A hedge fund manager identifies the historical prices of bonds A and B. The spread between the two prices has been relatively consistent over the last several years, but a recent event with one company has caused the price for bond A to decline. The hedge fund manager discovers this and buys bond A and simultaneously sells short bond B. Later on as the company that issued bond A recover from the event, the price increases and the hedge fund profits.

In the previous example, the hedge fund manager could have simply purchased bond A which was experiencing price declines and profited when the bond recovered in price as the company recovered. However, by not simultaneously selling short bond B, the hedge fund manager would leave the investment open to market exposure. That means that the profitability of the investment would depend on more than just the company recovering, but now must depend on how well or poorly the market performs. Under the fixed-income strategy, hedge fund managers want to isolate security-specific risk and eliminate or minimize market risk. To accomplish this goal, they sell short another fixed-income security. That way, when the market moves the price of a fixed-income security, both the long and the short positions, will offset each other. Isolating security-specific risk is thus accomplished. This strategy is very simple conceptually; hedge fund managers will scour the fixed-income marketplace to identify where the relationship between two or more securities is out of sync and then buy the undervalued security and sell the overvalued security. Identifying these out of sync abnormal relationships is no easy task of course.

As with convertible arbitrage and equity market neutral, fixed-income arbitrage does not care what the market is doing since good hedge fund managers will have hedged its inherent risk. Therefore, the source of risk and return for a fixed-income investment is entirely dependent on the security selected by the hedge fund manager. Profits under bull and bear market conditions can be made.

The most important factors impacting fixed-income prices and their yields include credit ratings, duration, coupon rate, and special bond provisions and features. Once issued, fixed-income prices can vary for any number of reasons, although the level of market interest rates is by far the most important of all factors. Another important factor includes the health of the issuer and its related credit rating. Credit ratings can change favorably or unfavorably depending on a company's current financial position and expected future positions.

Another advantage of fixed-income arbitrage is in their aim of profiting on pricing irregularities rather than on pure market interest rate plays. Interest rate investments speculate on the direction of interest rates while fixed-income arbitrage uses historical relationships between two fixed-income securities and current mispricings to make profits. Once the out of sync spread between the two fixed-income securities returns to more normal levels, the hedge fund will benefit.

As with the other relative value strategies, fixed-income arbitrage will oftentimes identify small, but investable opportunities. In consequence, hedge fund managers will typically employ large amounts of leverage to maximize profits.

Typical Risk: Low

Value Proposition: Reduced Volatility

Risk and Return Profile: Reduced Risk

Directional Bias: Both Net Long and Net Short

In the next chapter, you will learn about hybrid hedge funds, or those that combine multiple hedge fund strategies together to profit from any number of investment opportunities.

9

Hybrid Hedge Funds: A Balanced Style with Fund of Hedge Funds and Multi-Strategy

Now that we have discussed the three primary styles of hedge funds, we turn our attention to two hedge fund strategies that incorporate the other three hedge fund styles to some degree or another. These two hybrid strategies include multi-strategy and fund of hedge funds. This chapter will discuss both with more emphasis on fund of hedge funds, the fastest growing hedge fund style in the investment marketplace today. In 2002, it was estimated that there was close to 1200 fund of hedge funds. However, in 2003 alone, more than 500 new fund of hedge funds were established. This trend has continued since that time as more financial institutions, such as large banks, enter the trade and establish their own fund of hedge funds. Banks are making these moves to enhance product offerings to their wealth management clientele. Lastly, many estimates show that close to 40 percent of all new investment into hedge funds are flowing into fund of hedge funds. Suffice to say that knowing about fund of hedge funds is very important.

Please note that I use the description "fund of hedge funds" rather than the more common term "fund of funds." I use the previous term simply for learning purposes. Also, you may see the acronym FoF; this is short for fund of funds.

Multi-Strategy

A multi-strategy hedge fund strategy is a strategy whereby the hedge fund manager employs two or more strategies at one time or different times. Depending on the aim of the hedge fund manager, two strategies may be employed with equal emphasis or three strategies may be employed where one strategy is given more emphasis. Overweighting or underweighting strategies is common as managers attempt to take advantage of opportunities. For instance, a certain hedge fund manager may believe that a macro-strategy coupled with using an aggressive growth strategy is ideal for taking advantage of current opportunities and profit from them. At the same time, another hedge fund manager may believe that employing two arbitrage strategies would best suit the hedge fund and generate the level of performance he or she desires.

The primary advantage of using a multi-strategy strategy is that the hedge fund will be managed in a more diversified manner. Thus, if one particular strategy is performing poorly, the other strategy may be performing well and offsetting the poorly performing strategy. The obvious disadvantage is that a hedge fund has more chances of using a strategy that will not work. The more strategies a hedge fund manager uses, the greater the chances that one will not work in the current investing environment. However, with that being said, hedge funds that offer more than one strategy offer greater diversification over other hedge funds that only offer one strategy. More diversification is generally more preferred than not.

Fund of Hedge Funds

With a fund of hedge funds, the hedge fund manager invests in two or more stand-alone hedge funds rather than directly investing in securities themselves. This strategy provides enhanced diversification from the combination of multiple asset classes and multiple hedge funds. Fund of hedge funds emphasizes long-term performance with minimal volatility.

To take advantage of different opportunities, fund of hedge fund will periodically rebalance. This involves liquidating some positions in

Strategy	% of Funds
Equity Hedge	25%
Macro-centric	19%
Relative Value Arbitrage	15%
Event-Driven	12%
Fixed-Income Arbitrage	8%
Convertible Arbitrage	6%
Equity Nonhedge	4%
Distressed Securities	4%
Equity Market Neutral	3%
Sector Specific	2%
Merger Arbitrage	2%
Emerging Markets	2%
Short Selling	0%

Figure 9-1   Allocation of Multi-Strategy Assets

one or more hedge funds and making an investment in one or more other hedge funds. Rebalancing can be done to reduce the exposure to a particular hedge fund style or strategy within that style. In addition, rebalancing could be done to enhance exposure to a specific geographic area or to take advantage of risk reducing opportunities with a hedge fund that has a low correlation with the total fund of hedge funds portfolio.

Fund of hedge funds are the latest and greatest hedge fund offering. They are the new breed of hedge funds that has the entire industry buzzing. Fund of hedge funds pool money from client-investors and then invests that money in any number of other hedge funds that invest directly in securities. There are many benefits and advantages with fund of hedge funds with few drawbacks. Given the general lack of investor familiarity with hedge funds and how they operate, hedge fund managers of fund of hedge funds have the means to identify hedge funds that are the right fit for client-investors.

Benefits and Opportunities

Managers and other key people in the hedge fund management team with fund of hedge funds recognize the differences among hedge funds. In consequence, these managers blend various strategies and asset

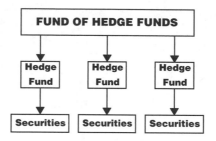

Figure 9-2   Fund of Hedge Funds Structure

classes together to generate attractive long-term investment returns while at the same time delivering lower investment volatility than the individual hedge funds that comprise the fund of hedge funds. Given this professional management and expertise, the following are the benefits and opportunities inherent in funds of hedge funds.

Provides for a Diversified Portfolio of Uncorrelated Hedge Funds

Managers of fund of hedge funds recognize that investing in two or more hedge funds is a good thing for diversification purposes. This lowers the total risk of the fund of hedge fund portfolio. However, these managers also recognize that investing in two or more hedge funds that are essentially the same provides little or no incremental benefit. As a result, fund of hedge fund managers target hedge funds that are fundamentally different from one another. This means that the correlation of the funds will be low, if not negative. The result to the portfolio is enhanced return and reduced risk. Individual investors have little knowledge in the way of which hedge funds provide correlation benefits. Fund of hedge funds can provide this advantage quickly and easily.

Provides Enhanced Diversification

Fund of hedge funds not only invest in multiple hedge funds, but also in asset classes, sectors, and geographic regions that are varied and different. In doing so, the fund of hedge funds will provide greater diversification, which leads to enhanced return and reduced risk. Multi-strategy hedge funds can also deliver this diversification aim as well, but fund of hedge funds is able to accomplish this task much easier given operational efficiencies.

Strives for More Consistent Returns

The aim is to deliver more consistent returns than stock portfolios, mutual funds, unit investment trusts (UITs), or individual hedge funds. Funds of Hedge funds generate more stable total returns under most market conditions due to the manager's ability and willingness to employ important investment management strategies.

Provides More Predictable Returns

Given that fund of hedge funds invest in multiple hedge funds, the predictability of hedge fund returns rises. This is simply the outcome of investing in multiple hedge funds. Although the return for each single hedge fund may change from period to period, the average of those returns will change much less. This translates into more predictable and consistent returns. Hedge funds with more predictable and consistent returns are more ideal since investors know what to expect.

Preferred Choice of Institutions

People who run pension funds are not experts with hedge funds. Although they know a great deal about investing, they also realize there is much to learn about hedge funds. At the same time, these professionals appreciate the value proposition fund of hedge funds offer. As a result, most institutions prefer and use fund of hedge funds for their hedge fund investments. These institutions include pension funds, endowments, insurance companies, private banks, and high net worth individuals and families.

Provides Access to Hedge Funds Otherwise Unavailable

One of the most significant benefits of fund of hedge funds is their access to hedge funds that are otherwise unavailable for investment purposes. Fund of hedge funds provide access to a broad range of styles, strategies, and hedge fund managers. They allow access to a broader spectrum of leading hedge funds that may otherwise be unavailable due to high minimum investment requirements. They also offer an ideal means to gain access to talented investment professionals, for a relatively modest minimum investment.

Provides Enhanced Diversification for Total Investment Portfolios

Not only do fund of hedge funds provide diversification for hedge fund investments, they also provide enhanced diversification for an investor's overall portfolio. A hedge fund portfolio should not be thought of as a stand-alone investment, but rather as a component to a larger portfolio.

Reduces Single Fund and Single Manager Risk

Funds of hedge funds minimize the risk associated with investing in one single hedge fund or hedge fund manager. This provides a safeguard to the portfolio to ensure that no single blowup with any hedge fund or hedge fund manager will severely impact the portfolio.

Eliminates the Time-Consuming Hedge Fund Due Diligence

Investing in hedge funds is not like investing in stocks or bonds or even investing in mutual funds. Investors need to exercise caution and due diligence with their investing decisions, including monitoring of hedge fund managers. Fund of hedge funds can accomplish much of this same work for the investor by making hedge fund investment decisions. Fund of hedge funds offer easier administration for a variety of hedge funds.

Performance of Fund of Hedge Funds

The performance of fund of hedge funds depends exclusively on the hedge funds the fund holds in the portfolio. Since the fund of hedge funds does not invest in securities directly, risk and return are generated from the component hedge funds. When the component hedge funds are doing well, the fund of hedge funds is doing well. Likewise, when the component fund of hedge funds is doing poorly so too will the fund of hedge funds. What is the big lesson here? The big lesson is that the performance of the fund of hedge funds depends on the skill of the manager in selecting appropriate component hedge funds.

Research has shown that fund of hedge funds and component hedge funds in general have performed rather equally over the same time periods. However, the real benefit as concluded by researchers is reduced levels of risk. Given enhanced diversification with fund of hedge funds, this is not necessarily unexpected. Rather, one of the defining characteristics of fund of hedge funds is the reduced risk. It is for this reason that fund of hedge funds are becoming so very popular.

In addition to reduced levels of risk, fund of hedge funds also provide lower correlations with the overall market, but more importantly, with the hedge fund market as a whole. Thus, investors in fund of hedge funds will experience return enhancing and risk reducing benefits.

Fees Associated with Fund of Hedge Funds

Fund of hedge funds charge the same two fees as do stand-alone hedge funds. These fees include the traditional management fee based on the level of assets under management and a performance incentive fee, which is a fee charged against the profits made in a particular year. Since fund of hedge funds do not actively invest in individual securities as stand-alone hedge funds, they do not charge the same fees as well. The typical stand-alone hedge fund will charge an annual investment management fee of between 1 and 2 percent and performance incentive fees of 20 percent. These numbers vary slightly from hedge fund to hedge fund, but are relatively the same for the trade. Funds of hedge funds charge an equal investment management fee of between 1 and 2 percent. Research shows that most charge close to 1 percent of the assets under management. Thus, investors with $1 million portfolios under management will incur a fee of $10,000 each year for the investment management fee.

Fund of hedge funds also charge the performance incentive fee, although much less than stand-alone hedge funds. The typical fund of hedge funds charge is between 10 and 12 percent, which is nearly half of what stand-alone hedge funds charge. Practically all fund of hedge funds that charge a performance incentive fee, and not all do, have high-water mark provisions. This protects the investor from paying the performance incentive fee twice on the same gains. Some fund of hedge funds do have hurdle provision safeguards, but for the most part they do not. For those that do offer hurdle rate provisions, the index of choice is LIBOR, or the London Interbank Offered Rate. Some other fund of hedge funds managers will elect to use the rate of Treasury Bills, which are short-term bonds that mature in less than 90 days and are issued by the United States government. Treasury investments are considered the safest of all investments in the global marketplace. But as we know, risk and return are related. This means that Treasury investments are the lowest returning investments in their particular maturity group.

Challenges and Drawbacks

With fund of hedge funds, there are three primary drawbacks. First, fund of hedge funds charge fees atop the fees already charged by the component hedge funds. Thus, component hedge funds will charge the customary investment management fee of 1 to 2 percent and a 20 percent performance incentive fee. At the same time, the fund of hedge funds will also charge the 1 to 2 percent investment management fee and tack on an additional 10 to 12 percent performance incentive fee. The net result is something like a 2 to 4 percent – average around 2.5 percent – investment management fee and a 30 percent performance incentive fee. There is no doubt that this two-tier fee structure is not appealing to investors. Thus, investors need to be cautious with investing in fund of hedge funds, but remember that it is the net result that matters, not the gross return and the fees charged. I'd rather pay 30 percent fees if my gross return were 25 percent than pay 10 percent fees for a gross return of 11 percent.

The second drawback is the lack of transparency, or lack of disclosure information. As with most hedge funds, there is a serious lack of information disclosure on the type of strategies in use and the assets held in the fund. However, this is changing as the hedge fund marketplace becomes more competitive and regulators continue breathing down the necks of hedge fund managers. Fund of hedge funds are no different from stand-alone hedge funds. They too offer little in the way of information disclosure. As a result, client-investors will have to take leaps of faith when investing in fund of hedge funds. Even though many fund of hedge funds do not provide the level of transparency that investors would like, that does not necessarily mean that something is foul. All is typically fine with how the fund is being run.

The third primary drawback of fund of hedge funds is reduced liquidity – since even more so than what is present with the component hedge funds. Funds of hedge funds need extra time to liquidate positions. Component hedge funds are not especially liquid investments themselves. Fund of hedge funds only magnify this characteristic. Most hedge funds have lock-up provisions of one year for new money into the fund.

Thereafter, hedge funds only allow withdrawals quarterly or annually. Some do provide for monthly withdrawals, but this is not common. As an investor in stand-alone hedge funds, fund of hedge funds are required to follow these same liquidity provisions. Many fund of hedge funds institute more stringent liquidity provisions. The most common provisions include lock-up provisions of one year for new money and six to twelve month redemption periods. The vast majority of fund of hedge funds do not allow for quarterly withdrawals. Some allow for monthly withdrawals but will charge a redemption penalty of 2 percent. Now that's motivation to stay in the fund and redeem per the guidelines set in the agreement. Lastly, some fund of hedge funds have liquidity gate provisions. These provisions restrict the amount that can be withdrawn from the fund at any one redemption time. This provision is used to safeguard against mass client-investor defections due to failing funds. Without doing so, the last investors could be stuck with nothing left. Slightly similar to a run on banks.

Menu of Fund of Hedge Funds

As with stand-alone hedge funds, fund of hedge funds also come in many forms. In general, there are four different types of fund of hedge funds. These four types of fund of hedge funds, including which stand-alone hedge funds they target, are provided below:

- *Conservative fund of hedge funds*: These funds invest in stand-alone hedge funds that use equity market neutral, fixed-income relative value, and arbitrage strategies
- *Long-biased fund of hedge funds*: These funds invest in stand-alone hedge funds that use tactical strategies
- *Defensive fund of hedge funds*: These funds invest in stand-alone hedge funds that use negative correlation, managed futures, or selling short strategies
- *Diversified fund of hedge funds*: These funds invest in stand-alone hedge funds that use lower volatility and multi-style strategies

Most hedge funds target only one type of stand-alone hedge fund. Thus, arbitrage fund of hedge funds will target arbitrage stand-alone hedge funds. At the same time, macro-centric fund of hedge funds target macro-centric hedge funds. This keeps operations and investment decisions quick, disciplined, and easy. Even within the different styles, fund of hedge funds can offer differing levels of sophistication and varying degrees of expertise and experience. Oftentimes investors will not be

Year	Assets in Billions
1997	$55
1998	$66
1999	$83
2000	$109
2001	$155
2002	$188
2003	$286
2004	$489

Figure 9-3   Assets Managed By Fund of Hedge Funds

aware of a particular fund of hedge fund's style or strategies targeted. Nevertheless, this enhanced focus provides investors with greater expertise and more options.

Summary of Investing Considerations

Even with the drawbacks inherent in fund of hedge funds, these funds provide an effective way for investors to invest in hedge funds. As mentioned previously, the benefits of enhanced diversification for investors and the benefit of allowing smaller investors the opportunity to invest in hedge funds can oftentimes outweigh the drawbacks. For some this is the case and for some this is not the case. Other benefits such as access to otherwise unavailable managers and the expertise and management of fund of hedge fund managers can make all the difference in the world. In contrast, for more experienced investors that have the capital necessary to hold multiple stand-alone hedge funds, bypassing the fund of hedge funds hybrid style can be a smart move. This will require greater funds to invest in each hedge fund and more time and effort to oversee and monitor how well each is performing.

One good source of information on fund of hedge funds can be found at www.hedgeworld.com. This website provides basic information on each fund and can be used as a starting point in your preliminary search for a fund of hedge funds.

In the next chapter, you will learn about the unique challenges of hedge funds, specifically the imposing legal and regulatory constraints that can preclude some investors from investing in hedge funds.

PART THREE

BUILDING A HEDGE FUND PORTFOLIO

Hedge Fund Challenges: Demystifying the Unique Legal and Regulatory Constraints

Now that we have discussed some of the big picture items investors need to consider when screening hedge fund managers, we turn our attention to the more specific challenges hedge fund investing presents. The basic challenges that we will focus on include legal and regulatory constraints. These are the very constraints that hedge funds must incorporate and investors must understand before making the initial investment. Chapter 11 continues the discussion of operational issues with a look at even more specific information unique to hedge funds, that being historical returns, risks, fees charged and tax implications.

Understanding the operational aspects of hedge funds is important since hedge fund managers may use any number of different legal structures to form the entity. These legal entities can be a limited partnership, a limited liability company, a commodity pool or even perhaps an offshore fund. Separate accounts for those who qualify can also be used.

The following context discuss common issues relating to challenges with hedge funds, specifically onshore hedge funds. Thereafter is a section on offshore hedge fund challenges.

Legal Organization

Mutual funds and hedge funds each establish quite different legal entities. However, they each have one goal in common at the organizational level, and that is the avoidance of tax implications at the fund level. As long as a certain amount of income in a mutual fund is distributed to investors, then the fund will not have to pay any taxes. Hedge funds do not want to incur taxes at the fund level either and they will not given that income flows directly to investors in the form of partnership interest. This is reported to each investor on a K-1 form.

The difference between the two is in the protection offered by the limited partnership status. Hedge funds establish themselves under partnership provisions to safeguard investors. Only the capital contributed by investors is at risk for loss as investors are limited partners. Hedge fund managers are the general partners of the hedge fund and stand to lose more that their capital contributed. However, many managers actually serve the role of the general partner as a company to limit the otherwise unlimited risk of loss.

It is not entirely accurate to say that hedge funds are unregulated investment pools. There are many regulations that hedge funds must adhere to, much like mutual funds. However, hedge funds are afforded the opportunity to take advantage of certain exemptions and exclusions to operate as a less regulated entity. Both mutual funds and hedge funds must comply with three laws relating to hedge fund investing. The first is the Investment Company Act of 1940. This regulation regulates and provides oversight for the investment offerings made to the general investing public. Hedge funds do not open up their funds to the general investing public, thus the impact of this regulation is minimal on hedge funds. Instead, hedge funds offer private placements to accredited investors. This means that hedge funds are regulated by what is called Regulation D of 1933 act.

Not only are hedge funds for the most part unregistered with the SEC, but also are the key people not registered. With mutual funds, the key people are duly registered, but that does not happen with hedge funds. This places greater restrictions on the ability of the hedge fund to market itself. Why does the SEC require both the funds and the key people to be properly registered? The reason is because the SEC takes aim at protecting and safeguarding the investing novice.

Number of Investors Constraints

Since mutual funds serve the general investing public, their goal is to serve as many investors as possible. Given that more assets under management translates into greater and increasing profits, mutual funds want large numbers of investors. Specifically, the SEC does not limit the number of investors that a mutual fund may manage, nor do they place restrictions on the size of investment each investor makes. Nevertheless, most mutual funds place minimum investment levels to ensure they are not losing money on a client. These minimums can range from $1000 to $2000. Once a mutual fund gets too large, the fund is typically closed to new investors. This protects the existing investors from lack of opportunities and dilution of opportunities presently being taken advantage of.

Hedge funds on the other hand, are not extended the same freedom in attracting whomever and however many investors as mutual funds. The SEC places harsh restrictions on the number and type of investors that can invest in hedge funds. The Investment Company Act of 1940 restricts the number of investors in unregulated investment pools, including hedge funds, to 100 or fewer investors. Furthermore, no public offering can be made by the fund. Advertising is forbidden. The second restriction placed on hedge funds as in Regulation D of the Securities Act of 1933 is that hedge funds can only accept accredited investors. Accredited is a fancy name for wealthy investor. Certain requirements must be satisfied according to the SEC. One such restriction limits institutions from investing in hedge funds unless that institution has $5 million or more in assets.

Liquidity Constraints

Mutual funds have no liquidity issues to speak of. Given their traditionally large size and diverse investor base, providing daily liquidity is not an issue with them. Hedge funds are an entirely different story. When dealing with the general investing public, the SEC requires investment funds, including mutual funds, to provide daily liquidity. This is not forced on hedge funds since they do not, or better said, cannot market or invest for the general investing public. This is both good and bad. Good for the reason that hedge funds are permitted to employ alternative investment strategies to profit from market inefficiencies and irregularities, but bad for the reason that they cannot market to a wider group of investors.

The sheer structure of a hedge fund prohibits daily liquidity. Since investors in hedge funds actually own an interest in the fund, liquidating that interest quickly is not especially easy. There are many hurdles that must be jumped, so-to-speak. In place of daily liquidity, hedge funds typically offer quarterly or annual liquidity. Some managers even require longer periods of time before invested capital can be liquidated. It is not unheard of for hedge fund managers to even require a multi-year lock-up period to ensure continuity of investing strategy. Backing off a strategy to satisfy a liquidity request will not make many hedge fund managers happy.

One quick note about mutual funds providing daily liquidity; only open-end mutual funds, or what make up the bulk of mutual fund investing by novice to intermediate investors, provide daily liquidity. Closed-end funds, which resemble index funds, do not offer direct shares of the funds – shares must be purchased on a national stock exchange. As a result, daily liquidity via the mutual fund is considered a non-issue.

Marketing Constraints

Marketing constraints? Mutual funds are provided with much greater freedom in marketing their product than are provides to hedge funds. In reality, mutual funds are restricted from some activities, such as claiming their fund will deliver a certain return over the next year, and required to carry out other activities, such as the disclosures made at the bottom of marketing slicks in magazines. These disclosures basically tell investors that there is a probability they can lose money by investing in the mentioned investment. Somewhat of a waste as investors already know this fact.

Mutual funds are permitted to market many things that hedge funds are not allowed to market. For instance, mutual funds are allowed to market investment results, investment holdings and philosophy for managing the fund. These important considerations can be marketed directly to the general investing public or to intermediaries, such as financial advisors and bank representatives that ultimately market to the general investing public. Either case, mutual funds have much greater flexibility in marketing than do hedge funds.

Hedge funds in contrast are not permitted to market the same information or market using the same ways. Hedge funds are restricted from marketing in newspapers, magazines and on television. In addition, hedge funds are not permitted to discuss investment performance or like information. Disclosing this information is permitted when a hedge fund manager is communicating with an accredited investor. This is permitted by the SEC. As a result, hedge fund managers are out of sight to most investors, except for those that know the benefits of hedge fund investing and actively seek out information on hedge funds.

Hedge fund managers do have ways in which they can market their funds. The primary methods are word of mouth and referrals. Other approaches include public relations activities that comply with the SEC. These activities may include television interviews or perhaps newspaper articles where the hedge fund manager is quoted. Nevertheless, hedge funds face an upward battle in their pursuit of marketing their funds to potential clients.

Custody Differences

Although a relatively non-issue with investors, custody is a big difference between mutual funds and hedge funds. Mutual funds are required to custody investor assets at banks while hedge funds are not. Given the type of investment strategies hedge funds employ, brokerage accounts provide the best way to custody investor assets. Regardless of the custody type, investors will not be impacted by this decision.

Distribution Constraints

In order for mutual funds to be classified as "pass-through" entities, 95 percent of the income received by the mutual fund must be distributed to investors. If a mutual fund fails to achieve this level of distribution, then the mutual fund itself will have to pass taxes on the income received. This is definitely not what mutual funds want to see happen. Investors have a choice to make when they receive distributions of income. They can either elect to take the distributions or reinvest the distributions back into the mutual fund. Most people reinvest the distributions back into the mutual fund, but some elect to take the distribution as they rely on the liquidity to support their living expenses. Regardless of the manner in which investors elect to receive their income, taxes must be paid. Yes, taxes must still be paid even if the distribution is not received and reinvested back into the fund.

Hedge funds differ slightly from mutual funds in this regard. Given the partnership legal structure, hedge funds are not required to distribute 95 percent of their income. Actually, they are not required to distribute any income. As a result, just about every hedge fund withholds income and instead reinvests the income back into the investments the hedge fund has going. This can be good for the investor since the hedge fund manager may be able to reinvest the money and make greater profits. Regardless, however, investors will still be required to pay taxes on the income, much like investors in mutual funds, even if they do not receive the money.

Incentive and Investment Management Fees

Mutual funds charge the standard investment management fee, which can vary depending on the type of mutual fund. Global mutual funds typically charge the highest percentages with bond funds charging some of the lowest fees. Contrary to what many investors know and think about mutual funds, mutual funds are permitted to charge a small incentive fee. This is called the fulcrum fee by the IRS. Under this scenario, mutual fund managers can receive a small percentage of the profits earned by each client. The incentive fee is nowhere near the 20 percent charged by hedge funds and typically is less than 1 percent. Most mutual funds do not subscribe to this way of investing given the drawback. The drawback of the fulcrum fee is that mutual funds must also take the bad with the good. This means that mutual funds are required to share in the losses the same way they share in the gains. The SEC does reward good investment returns, but also penalizes for poor investment returns. For this very reason, most mutual funds do not subscribe to this provision and instead do not participate in gains or losses.

Hedge funds on the other hand do not have to be concerned about sharing in both the gains and losses of a client. Hedge funds are permitted to go beyond the typical incentive fee relationships used by mutual funds and instead use the 1 and 20 arrangement. This arrangement simply means that hedge funds charge a standard 1 percent annual investment management fee, but also charge a 20 percent incentive fee. Hedge funds use hurdle rates and high-water marks to protect and safeguard investor assets. Mutual funds for the most part do not use these safeguard provisions.

Turnover Constraints

Prior to 1998, mutual funds were required to adhere to a strict regulatory constraint regarding turnover of a fund's assets called the "short short rule." This rule said that to avoid extra tax on realized gains, no more than 90 percent of total annual realized gains can come from positions held less than 90 days. In essence, this rule forbid mutual funds from short-term trading. An obvious good thing. In 1998, however, this rule was repealed and now mutual funds have greater latitude in making sell decisions. Market timing has become more popular as a result. Even given this change in rules, mutual funds still are motivated to hold positions for more than 90 days since the taxable rate for short-term gains and long-term gains is different. As a result, mutual funds recognize the advantage of holding positions longer than one year and take that into consideration when managing their funds.

Hedge funds on the other hand do not have these or any other restrictions on when to buy or sell securities. The gains or losses on hedge funds are treated the same way as mutual funds for short-term or long-term tax rates. Even though the playing field has been lowered, hedge funds still have higher turnover than mutual funds simply given their investment strategies. Hedge fund managers justify this by focusing on the net return. As long as the net return for a fund with higher turnover is better than the net return for a fund with lower turnover then hedge fund managers, or even mutual fund managers in this regard, have done their job. Gross return does not mean much with investing, it is only the net return or what you actually earn after taxes and fees that really counts.

Investment Constraints

Since mutual funds target the general investing public, the SEC limits the amount of risk that mutual funds can assume. These limits include restrictions on the amount of debt mutual funds can incur and how diversified mutual funds should be. The SEC specifically states that a mutual fund's gross exposure, which is defined as the gross long positions plus the gross short positions, cannot exceed 150 percent of a mutual fund's net assets under management. To promote diversified funds, the SEC limits the amount each fund can invest in any one company or industry and what percentage of the total market capitalization of a single company can own. If mutual funds do not comply with these SEC limitations, then they must market themselves as non-diversified funds. As you can image, mutual funds do not want to do this since they are all about gaining assets and this label surely will not help in accomplishing this goal.

Hedge funds on the other hand do not have to adhere to the same SEC restrictions regarding gross exposure nor limits on the degree of investing in any one company or industry. Some hedge funds are actually heavily invested in one or two assets. Macro-centric hedge funds are managed in this way. They typically over-emphasize one or more investments. If that investment does well then they will generate nice performance. But if not, then the fund will suffer.

Hedge funds do have to follow some of the rules mutual funds must follow with regard to margin requirements in order to leverage their funds. These margin requirements involve how much assets must be placed as a down payment to borrow. Regardless of whether or not the fund is a mutual fund or hedge fund, both still have to follow the same requirements regarding margin down payments. Margin requirements are imposed by the Federal Reserve and not the SEC.

Board of Directors

The SEC requires that mutual funds establish a board of directors for each mutual fund they operate. These boards of directors help to oversee fund management teams and are charged with promoting the interests of the mutual fund shareholders. To foster an objective and unbiased board, the SEC requires that a certain number of the board members come from outside of the fund and be totally independent of the fund's management team.

Hedge funds do not have to follow the same requirements as mutual funds with having boards. As a result, most hedge funds do not have boards of directors, although some do have an advisory board. This is not required either and the members of the advisory board do not have fiduciary duties like mutual fund board of directors have.

Challenges with Offshore Hedge Funds

Many people believe that offshore hedge funds are established to avoid paying United States taxes. This is absolutely not the case at all. In fact, taxable U.S. investors are essentially restricted from investing in offshore hedge funds. Furthermore, hedge funds do not assemble and distribute the needed forms to file tax returns for investors of offshore funds. If you do not have the required forms, you simply cannot invest in this type of hedge fund.

The only types of investors permitted in these funds include tax-exempt U.S. investors, such as pension plans, and non-U.S. investors, such as Canadian citizens. Why then are offshore funds established? They are established as a means to circumvent the rules regarding disclosure of information to investors. Many nations in the Caribbean promote themselves to hedge fund managers as places to setup shop. The fees these nations earn from hosting hedge funds can be quite lucrative for them.

Anticipated Changes and Future Regulation

If there is one guarantee hedge fund managers can make, it is that regulators will continue to target hedge funds and attempt to impose additional regulations on them. Regulators do not like hedge funds, which is basically alright as hedge fund management teams do not especially like the regulators. Regulators feel that hedge funds need significantly more restrictions placed on them, while hedge funds believe the regulators need a hands-off approach since mutual funds are already regulated and thus having mutual funds and hedge funds gives investors more options and opportunities. Regardless, one thing is for certain, regulators will continue to scrutinize hedge funds now and in the future. Perhaps one day when hedge funds morph into mutual funds or they simply do not exist, regulators will be satisfied and pat themselves on the back for a job well done.

The burden of policing hedge funds is quite substantial given the thousands that exist onshore and offshore. Regulators know this and have been focusing a good deal of their time on large financial institutions that lend money to hedge funds. Since leverage and the resulting higher risk is a significant factor in hedge funds downfall, regulators have pushed for greater scrutiny from large financial institutions on lending money to hedge funds. The markets themselves have recognized this necessity and tightened up on their lending practices without the influence of regulators.

One potential drawback of increased regulation is that investors will misjudge hedge funds and believe they are now less risky than before the regulation. As a result, some investors who should not be investing in hedge funds will do just that. In addition, some investors will become overconfident and invest more risky than they should. Both scenarios are not what the regulators want to see happen. This perceived lower risk of hedge funds is not ideal for the system as well. Risk and return are central to investing. Without this relationship and without the opportunity to invest in securities with high risk, investors will not be able to earn correspondingly high returns. A balance must be struck between safeguarding the general investing public and promoting a free investing marketplace.

═══════════════════════

In the next chapter, you will learn about the dynamics of hedge fund discovery for conducting an effective search for a hedge fund manager and evaluating the important factors of return, risk, fees and taxes.

11

Evaluating Hedge Funds: Screening and Assessing Performance, Risk, Fees, and Taxes

Today there are more than 9000 hedge funds in operation with more being established each and every day. This significant number creates logistical challenges for practically all investors, novice and advanced included. As a result, investing in hedge funds requires a good deal of effort and due diligence to screen out poor hedge fund managers and identity the ideal hedge fund managers to work with.

The task of manager discovery is a significant step unto itself and should not be approached lightly. As with investors and their objectives and constraints, hedge fund managers also differ in their backgrounds, expertise, philosophy, processes, strategies employed and performance track record. Hedge funds also differ with regard to risk, fees and taxes incurred. With so many alternatives to select from, the process can seem daunting. Remember, not all hedge fund managers are equal! Some managers may say the same things as others, but when you investigate further you will discover significant differences.

As with any other investment, establishing your goals and objectives is the logical first step with investing in hedge funds. Doing so will enhance the probability of achieving your investment goals. To properly locate and evaluate hedge fund managers, you will need to perform some basic information gathering, ask some specific questions and then spend time evaluating these hedge funds for proper fit.

Some of the factors you will need to investigate include assets under management, expertise of the hedge fund manager, strategies employed by the hedge fund manager and the instruments and tools used to initiate the strategies selected. After evaluating this data, certain managers will be eliminated while others will warrant additional investigation. This investigating will uncover many unique management styles and circumstances that either meets your goals or not.

Hedge Fund Information

Years ago, obtaining information on hedge funds was very difficult. Investors had to rely on contacts and referral sources for information. This has changed with the popularity of hedge funds growing exponentially. The hedge fund industry is a well-connected network of professionals who make gathering and disseminating information much easier than in the past. Word-of-mouth still continues to be the favorite source of investors seeking hedge fund investments. Given the restrictions on hedge fund marketing, this approach seems to work for both investor and manager. With the advent of rating services becoming involved in ranking hedge funds, the source of information will grow. Another solid source of information can be obtained from brokerage firms. These firms often times host seminars on hedge fund investing and invite hedge fund managers to give quick talks about their funds. Investors may find this venue a good fit. Websites such as HedgeWorld.com and PerTrac2000.com provide research on hedge funds for a fee. Over time more sources of information will surface providing additional help to the small and new hedge fund investor.

Gathering information on hedge funds begins with obtaining their offering memorandum, disclosure documents and legal partnership form. Some of these documents will prove beneficial in learning more about each hedge fund, but many will not due to the lack of disclosure. Such questions that are sometimes answered in these documents include:

1. What is the minimum initial investment?
2. What is the annual management fee and incentive performance fee?
3. What is the hurdle rate, if any?
4. Is there a water-mark provision?
5. What are the provisions for making withdrawals?
6. When can additional contributions be made?
7. How and when are performance and holdings communicated?
8. What strategies are employed and what is the stated goal?

Obtaining all other information, whether past or present, is vitally important. This will help you to ascertain the future expectations for the funds under review. Reviewing this information is best using two approaches – qualitative and quantitative. Under the qualitative approach, a review of the hedge fund management team is performed. This will uncover some unique strengths and some previously unknown weaknesses. Much can be learned by looking at the management team. Under the quantitative approach, you will want to review the performance, fees, taxes, and all other relevant numerical data of the hedge fund. This will paint a profound picture of the hedge fund and give you the much needed ammunition for making a decision on whether or not to invest.

This chapter is divided into two primary sections. The first section concentrates on hedge fund alternatives and talks about the four central considerations of hedge funds. The second section concentrates on hedge fund managers themselves. This second section provides a good list of questions you may want to investigate and ask hedge fund managers before making the initial investment.

Central Hedge Fund Considerations

During the hedge fund evaluation stage, you will want to concentrate your efforts on four central considerations. These considerations are specific to the hedge fund itself rather than dealing with the manager. The four central considerations include returns, risks, fees and taxes. We will explore each one of these over the next few pages.

Hedge Fund Performance

The process of screening hedge funds should begin with hedge fund performance. Note that I used the word performance rather than the word return. Return implies a rate of growth, such as 11 percent capital appreciation or 4 percent dividend yield. Performance on the other hand goes a step further. Here, returns are considered in the context of the goal. Thus, an 11 percent return is evaluated in the context of a forecasted 14 percent rate of return.

Screening for performance will help to automatically eliminate the bad from the good. Obtaining a complete and accurate performance track record is not easy to obtain, thus this process should be considered only a preliminary screening step. Some of the areas where you will want to concentrate the bulk of your time and resources include historical returns, dispersion of returns, and consistency of returns. Each will give you a solid look inside the performance of a hedge fund.

Historical returns demonstrate how well or poorly a hedge fund has done in the past. As we all know, past performance is not an indicator of future performance. Given that hedge fund managers possess a high degree of influence over a hedge fund, knowing past performance gives some indication of how the fund is managed. Are the returns all over the board or are they fairly consistent? Are the returns meeting the hedge fund's objective of generating attractive absolute returns? Are the returns exceeding the hurdle rate? Once you know the strategy the hedge fund manager is employing to manage the fund, identifying the historical returns will help you evaluate how good a job the manager has done.

Dispersion of returns is best described as how the return of a single hedge fund compares against the average return of its peer group. This provides a big-picture view of the hedge fund. Be cautious of hedge funds with wide dispersions of returns around the peer average return. This could indicate a haphazard approach to managing the fund. Why? Because if the majority of hedge fund managers are experiencing returns of 12 to 15 percent each year, but a certain hedge fund is experiencing returns of 10 to 17 percent, then one must question the effectiveness in implementing and managing the same strategy that others are using to generate more consistent returns.

Dispersion of returns leads into the third area of discussion, consistency of returns. Ideal hedge funds demonstrate high levels of consistency, regardless of how well the peer group is performing. High levels of consistency provide security in future performance. The more consistent now, one can argue, the more consistent in the future. Of course, consistency itself as a screening tool is not enough. Hedge funds can have high levels of consistency with generating poor performance. That isn't an ideal hedge fund. Thus, the aim of hedge funds should be rephrased to generate attractive absolute returns with minimal dispersion and maximum consistency.

Issues with Performance Screening

Screening performance in the pursuit of identifying good hedge fund managers has two issues. First, with the growth in the number of hedge funds in the marketplace, the sample average returns used for comparison purposes contains more managers at the end of the holding period than it did at the beginning of the holding period. Second, the return data exhibits a survivorship bias. This bias, extremely prevalent with mutual funds, means that as the poorly performing funds close and drop out of the return data, the average return rises. This rise is purely cosmetic and biased.

Hedge Fund Risks

As with any other investment, hedge funds possess some form of investment-specific risk. Each investment has general risk such as market, industry and political. However, hedge funds do have additional unique risks. These risks include operational risk, fraud risk, regulatory risk, transfer risk, settlement risk, credit risk, legal risk, and liquidity risk. Depending on the hedge fund and type of strategy, an investor may be exposed to a couple of these risks or all of them. The degree of risk can also differ from hedge fund to hedge fund. Each of these risks is described as follows.

Operational Risk

Operational risk refers to the hedge fund company and the risks associated with not being able to manage the hedge fund as should happen. These risks include a lack of resources, technology problems, key people departures and even infrastructure insufficiencies. This could result in errors in valuing the hedge fund or in reporting taxable gains to investors.

Fraud Risk

Fraud is perhaps the most serious of all types of hedge fund risk. When investors place their trust in a hedge fund manager and invest in a fund, they are expecting the manager to behave and conduct themselves with integrity. Fraud can bring down an entire hedge fund and hedge fund company. When a hedge fund manager, or any other investment manager for that matter, does not act with integrity, then everyone loses.

Regulatory Risk

Regulatory risk refers to the current and future restraints imposed on hedge funds. These restraints include margin requirements, disclosure of information, registration of hedge funds, and number and type of hedge fund investors permitted to invest in hedge funds. The Federal Reserve requiring hedge funds – including other investment managers – to post greater margin, thus reducing leverage, would impact those hedge "funds that employ broad leverage."

Transfer Risk

Transfer risk refers to the restriction of transferring ownership interest from one hedge fund investor to another. Thus, hedge fund investors are required to liquidate their hedge fund investment directly with the fund itself. Although this risk is marginal, to some investors it can be quite important.

Settlement Risk

Settlement risk is the risk that a hedge fund will be unable to finalize a transaction at the terms of the contract agreed to on the purchase trade date. This risk is minimized for exchange traded instruments, but exists with off exchange instruments. Not settling at agreed upon terms can cost delays and perhaps require legal or arbitrary means to resolve.

Credit Risk

Credit risk refers to the risk arrising from a company that a hedge fund may "have invested" in which may declare bankruptcy or cease paying bond interest payments due to a challenging financial position. Since some hedge funds invest in fixed-income securities, there is always the risk that they could default on payments. If this were to happen, then the hedge fund could experience performance challenges.

Legal Risk

Legal risk refers to the risk that a hedge fund will face legal challenges that need the attention of the management team. Compliance to ensure all aspects of regulatory considerations are adhered to is also included. Lastly, addressing and resolving regulatory violations is also part of legal risk.

Liquidity Risk

Liquidity risk can refer to two things. First, this risk can refer to the risk where a hedge fund is unable to liquidate an investment at a price close to the present market value. Larger investment positions attempting to be sold can be especially challenging. In addition, since some hedge funds invest in relatively illiquid assets, selling these positions could take significant time and effort. For the investor, liquidity risk refers to the restrictions on withdrawing money from the hedge fund. Most hedge funds have restrictions on when money can be withdrawn, primarily only quarterly and not at all in the first year of the investment.

Strategy Risk

Strategy risk refers to the risk embedded in the strategies employed by the hedge fund manager. This includes the trading styles employed, the investment markets and industries the hedge fund targets and the specific investments selected and held in the hedge fund.

Hedge Fund Fees

Hedge funds typically charge two types of fees. These two include a fixed investment management fee and a performance incentive fee. The standard performance incentive fee is 20 percent, although some can be found that differ from this amount. This fee is charged on all gains, whether realized or unrealized, including sales of securities, dividends and interest payments received and appreciation of investments held. This fee is based on the total return of the fund. Investors will from time to time pay this fee only to see the value of their investment decline. To protect the investor from paying a fee for gaining that value back, hedge funds have high-water marks. These safeguards ensure that investor-clients do not pay fees twice for the same gain in value. For instance, suppose an investor contributes $1 million to a hedge fund and over the subsequent year, the investor earns 10 percent. The portfolio at the end of the year will then be $1.1 million. The high-water mark has now been set at $1.1 million. The hedge fund will charge the standard 20 percent performance incentive fee against the 10 percent earned, or $100,000. This will translate into a fee of $20,000. However, for simplicity, all value are gross of fees. Now suppose in year two the investment declines by $50,000, thus a value of $1.05 million at the end of year two. In year three the investment again experiences a 10 percent gain, or $105,000. The high-water mark provision will safeguard the investor from paying the performance incentive fee twice on the same value created. Given the high-water mark of $1.1 million, the investor will only incur a 20 percent fee, or $1,100. This amount is determined by taking the value of $1.1055 million in year three, subtracting the high-water mark value of $1.1 million, and plus multiplying by .2 for the performance incentive fee. The new high-water mark is now set at $1.1055 million and only gains above this amount will incur the performance incentive fee.

The 20 percent fee is commonly applied to the gain in value AFTER the standard 1 percent investment management fee is charged. For example, suppose an investor earns 14 percent in a particular year giving that investor $3 million in total value. The 1 percent investment management fee is then charged against the $3 million. This equates to $30,000. The performance incentive fee is then charged against the gain less the $30,000 investment management fee. Note that many hedge funds deduct the 1 percent fee prior to the performance incentive fee, but others do not. Some charge the performance incentive fee first followed by the investment management fee. The common investment management fee is charged to cover the operating expenses of the hedge fund. These expenses include accounting and auditing, payroll, marketing and compliance.

Another safeguard provision some hedge funds use is a hurdle rate. A hurdle rate is the point where performance above the rate is charged the performance incentive fee. Performance below the hurdle rate is not charged this fee. The hurdle rate is most always tied to a short-term rate, such as LIBOR. Rates such as the S&P 500 are not used since this would cause hedge funds to abandon their traditional investment strategies and instead become more focused on equity securities.

The use of fees all depends on the hedge fund. Some hedge funds charge performance incentive fees of more than 20 percent and some less. At the same time, some hedge funds charge the standard 1 percent investment management fee and some charge more and some less. The high-water mark and hurdle rate are also variable. Most hedge funds do operate with high-water mark provisions, but most do not have hurdle rates. Furthermore, hedge funds are typically willing to negotiate fees. The greater the assets that an investor brings, the greater the negotiating leverage that investor has.

One final note regarding performance incentive fees. Many people think that hedge fund managers try to maximize this fee by assuming high levels of risk. This is not the case for two simple reasons. First, the top hedge fund managers have their own money in their hedge funds. Thus, if they take too much risk with the fund they will put not only the assets of their investor-clients at risk, but also their own money. Second, hedge fund managers for the most part want to stay in this business long-term. Compensation generated over their lifetime is significantly more appealing than earning more in one year that is comparably less over time. For these reasons, hedge fund managers recognize the need to take calculated and smart risks. Doing so will help the investor and manager sleep better at night.

Hedge Fund Taxes

Hedge funds are considered "pass-through entities." This means that hedge funds themselves do not pay taxes, but instead pass all gains and losses to the individual investors. Since hedge funds typically engage in active trading, realized gains and losses are common. This translates to more challenging tax planning and reporting. Schedule K-1s, or Form 1065, is supplied to investors of hedge funds given that the limited partnership form is the structure of choice for hedge funds. K-1s are not due to investors until the tax deadline so investors will discover filing their taxes a chore in patience and discipline. Tax reporting extensions are frequent with hedge fund investors.

Limited partners, or the investors, receive capital gains and losses in proportion to their interest in a hedge fund. For instance, if an investor held a 10 percent interest in a hedge fund and that hedge fund generated $100,000 in capital gains for a tax year, then the investor will incur $40,000 in capital gains. Capital gains are taxed according to the investor's personal tax rates. As with mutual funds, investors are responsible for reporting earnings, both income and capital gains, even if the investor did not withdraw money from the fund. This is similar to the Phantom Tax that investors in certificates of deposit must pay even when their earnings are locked-up in the CD.

The frequency and amount hedge fund investors pay in taxes depend on the specific hedge fund and, more importantly, on the type of strategy employed by the manager. The actions of the hedge fund manager to carry out each said strategy will be a factor in any tax consequences generated. As previously mentioned, the degree of active trading is a big factor in tax implications. Selling existing investments will generate either capital gains or losses. Capital gains can be taxed in one of two ways. These include short-term gains or long-term gains. The tax rate on long-term gains is lower as it gives investors incentive to hold investments for more than a year rather than flipping to make a profit. Capital losses are offset against capital gains to minimize taxable consequences. However, there is a maximum capital loss amount that investors can report without offsetting against capital gains. A portion of excess capital losses, if existing, can be carried over to the next tax year and offset against capital gains.

The second type of tax hedge fund investors will incur is ordinary income tax. Ordinary income comprises the dividends and interest received from the holdings in the hedge fund. This type of income is received in the form of stock dividends and interest payments from bonds. Depending on the type of hedge fund, an investor may or may not be exposed to this tax consideration, but most will. Many stocks do pay dividends, so most investors will incur some taxes on current income.

Not only does the type of hedge fund make a difference in the taxes investors incur, but so too does the type of investor. Individual investors for the most part hold taxable portfolios. However, not-for-profit institutions are tax-exempt. Thus, tax considerations are not a significant issue with this type of investor. However, for the vast majority of investors, taxes are a priority issue as they can take a series bite out of your earnings. Remember, it is not what you earn when the day is all said and done, but rather what you take away and keep. Keep tax considerations at the forefront of your evaluation of hedge funds. Specifically ask the hedge fund management team about this consideration.

Hedge Fund Manager Discovery

Manager discovery and the pursuit of finding the ideal hedge fund manager is the key first step with investing in hedge funds. Regardless of your experience with investing, you need to ensure that some very basic and important tasks are followed for selecting a hedge fund manager. The following are some of the critical considerations you should investigate about each hedge fund manager before making the initial hedge fund investment.

Identify Hedge Fund Offerings

The first step you should undertake is to identify the various hedge fund offerings available to you. Do they offer high-risk high potential return hedge funds, low risk and low potential return hedge funds, or a combination of the two? Can the hedge fund manager integrate his offerings with the portfolio you presently have or will this be a stand-alone investment? Does the hedge fund manager offer multiple hedge funds to provide investors with a choice of strategy? Once the question of hedge fund offerings is answered, you then can make an informed decision on whether or not to go any further in your investigation of the manager. This initial step will help you avoid a problem in the future.

Investigate Hedge Fund Performance

Most hedge fund managers will provide you with some type of performance composite for you to review. When reviewing performance, be sure to learn which benchmark or benchmarks are employed, how well the manager performed against his or her peer group, how consistent performance has been over long periods of time, what type of volatility is typical in the hedge fund, what the growth of assets under management has been and how and when the performance composite was created. A statement claiming that the performance composite conforms to CFA Institute standards is your best assurance that the results are accurate. Some hedge funds even go a step further and have an external party review their performance composite and give it their stamp of approval. If any of these items are not provided, ask the manager to provide them.

Obtain Disclosure Documents

All onshore hedge funds are required to provide an offering memorandum, a limited partnership agreement and a subscription agreement. Make sure you understand the level of risk, the initial investment minimum, any withdrawal provisions and other important considerations. Evaluate this information within the context of your goals and objectives and ensure they are suitable with your investing goals, time horizon, and risk profile (tolerance, capacity, and need). As with any investment, the higher the potential returns for a given hedge fund, the higher the potential risk you must assume. Risk and return are linked.

Identify How and When the Assets in the Hedge Fund are Valued

To take advantage of unique opportunities, some hedge funds will need to invest in highly illiquid securities that may be difficult to value. In addition, many hedge funds exercise significant discretion in the method and timing of valuing securities. Make every effort to identify the timing of when the valuation will be performed (e.g. monthly, quarterly) and how the assets are valued. It is always wise to fully understand the valuation process and learn if the assets in the hedge fund are valued by an independent external source.

Investigate Fees

Fees have a big impact on your net return. Most hedge funds typically charge an investment management fee of 1 to 2 percent of assets under management, plus "a performance incentive fee," which is typically 20 percent of profits. This incentive performance fee is used to motivate the hedge fund manager to generate positive returns. If the hedge fund manager does not perform, then the investor will not have to pay. A win-win situation for both. At the same time, however, this incentive performance fee could motivate a hedge fund manager to take greater risks than warranted in pursuit of even greater returns, and thus more fees. Most hedge funds will charge both the annual investment management fee and the performance incentive fee. However, funds of hedge funds will typically charge only the annual investment management fee and not the performance incentive fee since the fund will already be exposed to this fee given that the fund invests in other hedge funds that do charge the fee. Note that some fund of hedge funds do charge an performance incentive fee. Remember to get all of this information on the table from the outset.

Uncover Restrictions on Redeeming Hedge Fund Interest

The vast majority of hedge funds typically restrict investors from redeeming their interest in hedge funds. These restrictions include the first year period of withholding the right to withdraw from the hedge fund to the periods of time when withdrawals can be made. Most funds include the first year provision where your investment is locked-up for a period of one year or more. Thereafter, funds are typically available only on a quarterly or annual basis. These provisions are instituted to give hedge fund managers the opportunities to employ their strategies and to give these managers the required time to liquidate investments to cover withdrawals from investments that are difficult to sell or otherwise illiquid.

Inquire About Tax Considerations

Some managers underemphasize tax management while other managers overemphasize it. Specifically, ask about the general degree of turnover, how they incorporate tax management into their management process and how they approach the issue of tax loss-harvesting and exchange strategies. Many hedge fund managers will strive to maximize the top line, or gross return, but the top managers will focus on maximizing the bottom line, or net return. Remember, if you cannot walk away with it, did you really earn it in the first place? That said, it does not quite matter if you earned a substantial return if you must turn around and give Uncle Sam a big chunk of that return.

Conduct a Background Check on the Hedge Fund Manager

This is perhaps the golden rule of hedge fund investing. Know with whom you are investing your money. Make sure the hedge fund manager and other key decision-makers are qualified to manage your money. Investigate what type of education the manager has – a bachelors or perhaps a masters degree? Investigate whether or not the manager has earned professional designations, such as the CFA (Chartered Financial Analyst), CPA (Certified Public Accountant), CFP® (Certified Financial Planner), or ChFC (Chartered Financial Consultant). Having a designation illustrates commitment and specialized knowledge, both of which separate the top managers from the rest of the pack.

Investigate how long the manager has been managing hedge funds and how much experience he or she has with investments and portfolio management. Also inquire how long the manager has been in his or her present role. You will find many hedge fund managers with very little experience with not only hedge funds, but also portfolio management. Given the lure of hefty compensation from the performance incentive fees, more and more people with little direct experience are entering this field. That does not mean that a manager with little experience will fail at generating attractive returns and meet goals and objectives, it only means that you should exercise extra caution.

Investigate Ethical Considerations

This step is obviously very subjective and not always easy to answer when you first meet a hedge fund manager. A good way to approach this questions is to investigate whether or not either a regulatory organization or a private association he or she might be a member of has publicly disciplined him or her. You can obtain this type of information by reviewing the manager's Form ADV-II, if available. Depending on whether or not this form is available, it may be possible for you to review the firm's Form ADV-II using the SECs Investment Adviser Public Disclosure (IAPD) website. For managers with less than $25 million in assets under management, the state securities regulator where the manager's principal place of business is located can provide this type of information. Lastly, you may find information from the NASD (National Association of Securities Dealers) or any association the manager is a member of, such as the Certified Financial Planning Board of Standards (www.CFP.net) or the CFA Institute (www.CFAInstitute.org).

Ask About the Manager's Personal Investments

Hedge fund managers should have a substantial amount of their invest-able assets in the hedge fund he or she is managing. Moreover, the hedge fund manager should not have any investments of similar type outside of the hedge fund. Inquire to the hedge fund manager about both of these questions. Exercise caution with hedge fund managers who invest actively in similar investments outside of the hedge fund he or she manages. Owning non-similar assets such as treasuries or real estate is not a concern as it does not cause conflicts of interest or signal better investments can be found outside of the fund. Hedge fund managers who invest a substantial amount of their personal assets in the fund will also have an extra incentive to generate attractive returns. This is a win-win for both involved and provides more confidence to the investor in knowing the interests of the manager and client are aligned. If hedge fund managers are investing outside of their funds, perhaps investors should do the same.

Consider the Personality Fit

Usually after the first meeting you will know if there is a fit or not. Is the manager more serious or humorous? Is the manager intense or low-key? Is the manager more professional or down-to-earth? Does he or she play golf? Did a friend refer you? Are your interests similar? Etc, etc. Personality fit is not a high priority item; however, not having a good relationship with your hedge fund manager will make things more difficult.

Do Not Be Afraid to Ask Additional Questions

Investing in hedge funds is not quite the same as picking stocks and bonds or investing in mutual funds. With hedge funds, you are entrusting your money to someone who wields a significant degree of freedom in making investment decisions impacting your portfolio. As a result, you should know where and how your money is being invested, who the key decision-makers are, what strategies will be employed, how and when you can redeem your investment or make additional contributions, what safeguards are in place to protect your investment and what your rights are as an investor.

Decision-Making

Evaluating a hedge fund manager based on the information you gathered in the interview and in researching the disclosure documents can be challenging at best. After speaking with the hedge fund management team, you may get a negative feeling and end the investigation right then. At other times you will get a positive feeling and decide to continue or perhaps invest at that point. Managers that are unable to answer simple questions about their hedge fund, the hedge fund company or the current and anticipated investing marketplace could be a signal for you to stop the process. As with experience in shopping for homes to purchase, gaining experience with investigating hedge fund managers is invaluable and will serve you well.

No single positive response should motivate an investor to select a certain hedge fund. That is unwise. However, one such negative response to any other of the items investors should investigate could, and perhaps should, motivate the investor to stop and move on to another hedge fund manager. Identifying the best hedge fund manager is a Herculean effort. Instead, focus on finding good hedge fund managers and select the one or more managers that best fits your needs and personality. It is smart to diversify your hedge fund managers rather than concentrating on only one. This will minimize manager-specific risk similar to how hedge fund managers minimize investment-specific risk by investing in numerous securities. Evaluating and selecting a manager is vitally important and should be handled with the utmost care, skill, and patience.

In the next chapter, you will learn about how to be successful in making your initial hedge fund investment.

12

Hedge Fund Investing: The Long and the Short of Making the Initial Investment

Now that you have evaluated a number of hedge funds and hedge fund management teams, you can focus on making the initial investment in a hedge fund or hedge funds. In this chapter we will expound on the previous chapter and discuss how to build a hedge fund portfolio. Specifically, this chapter will cover three important considerations for building a hedge fund portfolio. These three considerations include understanding your objectives and constraints, planning your hedge fund investment, and sensible strategies for successful hedge fund investing.

In order for you to achieve a successful hedge fund portfolio, you will first want to understand your objectives and constraints. These are very important since they dictate which hedge fund and hedge fund strategy is most important to you. This includes identifying your financial goals and defining your investment objective. Once you have accomplished this task, you will then select the hedge fund or hedge funds most appropriate to accomplish your investment objective. The last consideration in this chapter will provide finer detail on what you should think about prior to making your investment. These seven sensible strategies could mean the success or failure of your investment.

As with traditional investments, investments in hedge funds should be approached rationally and prudently. This process begins with making important decisions, and decisions that will ultimately impact how well your investment objectives are accomplished or not. For those investors with some experience with hedge funds, this process is relatively simple and straightforward; however, other investors will discover this process to be more challenging. Let's investigate what defines what type of hedge fund you should be seeking out.

Understand Your Objectives and Constraints

SMART Goals

Having investment goals and striving to attain those goals will give not only your hedge fund investing purpose, but also your overall investing direction and focus. Do you need money in two years for a new home or will you be receiving a lump sum retirement distribution perhaps? For investors that need more income in the form of interest and dividends or need greater liquidity in their portfolio, allocating a smaller amount to hedge funds is prudent. For investors that have no liquidity need or obligations, allocating a greater amount to hedge funds could be a wise strategy. To best identify your goals, investors should emphasize SMART financial goals. SMART is an acronym that best illustrates the five characteristics of well-designed financial goals, as follows:

- *Specific*: Your goals should be unambiguous, clear and well-defined.
- *Measurable*: Your goals should be quantifiable and calculable.
- *Accepted*: Your goals should be acknowledged and motivational.
- *Realistic*: Your goals should be achievable and attainable, not lofty.
- *Time-centric*: Your goals should be for a set period, nothing indefinite.

Investment Knowledge

Time and time again we hear "invest in what you know." Both Warren Buffet and Peter Lynch propagated this belief. The more knowledgeable you are about a specific investment the more confident and certain you are regarding whether or not that investment is appropriate and suitable. On the flip side, the less you know about an investment the more apprehensive and uncertain you are about whether or not to hold that particular investment in your portfolio.

All else held constant, the greater your investment knowledge the higher your risk tolerance. An investor with strong investment knowledge will typically have a portfolio with high-risk investments. On the flip side, an investor with weak investment knowledge will tend to design a portfolio with lower to moderate-risk investment holdings. Although identifying the assets in a hedge fund is not exactly easy, doing so will help in deciding if that fund is a good match.

Investment Objectives

The most common investment objectives investors tend to establish include protecting their portfolios and growing them well over time. In other words, earning a sufficient return. Return aspiration is the desired financial reward sought by you for deferring current consumption and making an investment. The reward for making an investment can come in two forms – appreciation of principle and receiving dividends and interest income.

The goal here is to gain a better perspective on what return it is going to take in order to achieve your SMART goals. Thus, you may need a slightly higher return to build a portfolio large enough to fund your retirement sometime in the future. Lastly, your return aspiration should be realistic, neither vague nor unattainable.

Current and Projected Financial Position

Your level of wealth will play a substantial role in determining your asset allocation. In general, investors with higher levels of wealth tend to have greater capacity for assuming risk. Simply put, wealthy investors have more room for error in achieving their goals. Of course this is not always the case, but as a general rule it usually holds true. For instance, if you were to win the lottery, your capacity to assume risk would increase dramatically. Wouldn't you care less about losing $50,000 if you just won $25,000,000?

Hedge funds investors, out of sheer screening due to SEC regulations, are in much better financial positions than other investors. However, hedge fund investors should take a good look at their current and projected financial position and identify what their loss capacity may be and determine the prudent amount to invest in hedge funds.

Risk Profile

Your risk profile is perhaps the most important investment consideration. Your risk profile will not only determine how you allocate your portfolio from the outset, but also how you manage your portfolio over time. Your risk profile is comprised of three similar, yet still separate, factors. These include your tolerance for risk, your capacity to assume risk and your need to assume risk. The lowest value in any one of the three factors is considered the maximum level of risk you should assume in your portfolio. For example, although an investor may have a high-risk tolerance and high capacity to assume risk, that investor may have a low need to assume risk. Why? The reason is because many investors do not have the need to assume risk since their wealth is more than adequate to fund their lifestyle and goals, now and in the future. Unfortunately, investor risk profile is difficult to measure for three reasons. First, risk is specific to the situation. Second, investment-specific risk is not easily understood and therefore people act irrationally and without predicta bility. Third, investor risk profile – tolerance, capacity, and need – changes over time, it is not static. Thus, your risk profile could be always moving, not easy to isolate, and difficult to accommodate, as a result.

Since you cannot control investment results, risk tolerance is therefore based on your tolerance for volatility. Investments with greater volatility have higher chances of experiencing price declines, which means you may not achieve your return aspiration.

Time Horizon

Not only is time horizon a key investing consideration, it is also a cornerstone principle of asset allocation, and rightfully so. Time horizon greatly impacts expectations for asset class returns, asset class volatility, and correlations among asset classes.

The primary use of time horizon is to help you determine the portfolio balance between equities and fixed-income, namely bonds and cash. All else being equal, the longer your time horizon the more equity assets and less fixed-income assets you should hold.

The most prevalent type of risk you need to address over the long-term is purchasing power risk, or the loss in an asset's real value due to inflation. Equity investments provide the best hedge against this type of risk. In the short-term, the most prevalent risk is price volatility. Fixed-income investments provide the best hedge against this type of risk.

Income and Liquidity Needs & Preferences

Your needs for current income and liquidity will impact how you allocate your portfolio, including investments in hedge funds. This consideration addresses the degree to which you require cash to accomplish everyday activities and make special purchases. Consider, for example, a retired couple who use their investment portfolio to fund their retirement. In this situation, the retired couple would have a much higher liquidity and income need than would a couple in their prime earning years where their income exceeds their expenses. As a result, the retired couple would need to build a portfolio that emphasizes income-oriented investments. Hedge funds may not be the smart investment in this scenario.

Tax Status and Tax Considerations

This consideration is central to deciding what asset classes to hold in your portfolio. One of the primary purposes is to aid in deciding what type of fixed-income securities to buy, namely taxable or tax-exempt. For taxable portfolios, investors with high federal tax rates will find it more appropriate to invest in tax-exempt investments rather than taxable investments. Tax-exempt portfolios should focus on taxable investments since the benefit of employing tax-exempt securities will be eliminated.

In addition to aiding in the decision to buy taxable or tax-exempt investments, this will assist in the complex project of realizing, deferring, and avoiding taxes for the benefit of your portfolio. In consequence, tax management has become one of the hot new buzz-words in portfolio management. Justifiably so since they can reduce portfolio performance by a substantial amount via capital gains taxes. In response, taxes and their impact on your portfolio should be one of your considerations when allocating your assets. As the number and complexity of your tax issues increase, so to does the need to involve either a CPA or an estate planning attorney.

Unique Preferences and Circumstances

This consideration essentially incorporates anything that cannot be categorized in one of the other inputs, but still impacts how you should allocate your portfolio. Many of the items incorporated in this input are uniquely specific to the individual investor. These items can range in depth and breadth and may not be common to other investors.

Planning the Hedge Fund Portfolio

As with traditional investing, smart decisions backed by thorough research is important with hedge funds. Having realistic goals and objectives is critical. For investors to have realistic goals and objectives, they must first understand basic investing lessons and prudent ways to manage their portfolios for long-term growth. But what are some of the benchmarks for hedge fund investing, in particular how much to invest in hedge funds and how many hedge funds to hold.

How Much in Hedge Funds

Determining how much to allocate to hedge funds is one of the most important questions with hedge fund investing. Unfortunately, this question is also one of the most subjective of hedge fund investing as well. The best response to give is that it all depends. It all depends on the type of investor, the risk profile of an investor, the time horizon of an investor, an investor's need for liquidity, an investor's return aspiration, and more. The aforementioned considerations provide a strong look inside what helps to determine how much to invest in hedge funds. Many investing gurus say that investors, depending on their level of wealth and risk profile, should allocate anywhere from 0 to 20 percent in alternative assets. Hedge funds are combined in the alternative asset class. However, remember that hedge funds are not really an asset class themselves, but rather a different strategy for investing. This approach has made people label them as alternative.

Allocating anywhere from 0 to 20 percent is the commonly held view with more traditional investment managers. However, many hedge fund mangers will say that allocations significantly higher than that figure should be considered. Some research has shown that allocations close to 60 percent should be invested in hedge funds. That is much too high for the typical hedge fund investor. Allocations somewhere between the two viewpoints is more appropriate. Allocations of 20 to 25 percent in hedge funds is not necessarily unwise. Given that hedge funds can exhibit conservative risk levels with low volatility, hedge fund allocations above traditionally held allocations of 20 percent or less can be achieved. The central aim therefore is how best to allocate the hedge fund investment once the allocation itself has been established.

How Many Hedge Funds

Again, it all depends. What level of portfolio diversification are you looking to achieve? What level of oversight are you willing and able to accommodate? With diversification, both the hedge fund management team and the strategies employed should be taken into consideration. Given the numerous hedge fund strategies available, investing in multiple hedge funds that employ different strategies will help to diversify your hedge fund portfolio. For example, you may invest in a hedge fund that employs a macro-strategy whereby the manager places bets on which direction the price of a specific market, sector, or investment will move in price. At the same time, that investor may want to incorporate a hedge fund that employs a distressed securities strategy. In doing so, the investor will incorporate investments that are more value-oriented and with a somewhat longer term time horizon. As with asset classes, at different points in time, different hedge fund strategies will do better than others. Investors with multiple hedge funds or hedge fund strategies will benefit from this rotation of which strategy is doing best. One good and easy solution to diversifying across multiple strategies is to invest in a hedge fund that employs multiple strategies rather than just one. Diversifying with two or more hedge fund managers is important when a multiple strategy hedge fund is held.

Research shows that investing in multiple hedge fund managers provides for more diversified and optimal hedge fund portfolios. As with the research relating to the allocation to hedge funds, research on the number of hedge fund managers to use is across the board. Some researchers indicate that over fifteen managers is most optimal. Doing so is simply not practical for individual investors, but is for institutional investors. The best advice is to consider more than one hedge fund manager and perhaps as many as five. Think of your mutual fund portfolio. Rarely do investors hold one or even two mutual funds. Some investors even hold upwards of fifteen mutual funds. Once you hit fifteen, you are maximizing diversification and even approaching a market portfolio. That is not especially wise since mutual funds charge higher management fees than index funds and at this point they are relatively the same thing.

Fund of hedge funds provides one of the best ways for investors to diversify across a broad number of hedge fund managers. The managers of funds of hedge funds are experts at knowing hedge funds, hedge fund management teams, and which is best to invest in with the fund. As a result, they offer one of the best ways to diversify both in terms of hedge fund strategies and hedge fund managers.

Seven Sensible Strategies for Successful Hedge Fund Investing

There are no guarantees with hedge fund investing and there are no shortcuts. Some investments are insured, but none are guaranteed. The same is true with hedge fund investing. As a result, some investors will have bad experiences with investing in hedge funds while many will have positive and beneficial experiences. To give you an idea of how best to maximize your opportunity to experience a successful hedge fund investment, I have provided the following sensible strategies.

Strategy 1: Do Your Preliminary Background Research and Do it Well

Managing your portfolio always begins with you. Selecting a hedge fund manager or hedge fund based on a recommendation from a friend or advisor is not good enough. Investors need to take a more proactive role in screening hedge funds and managers and then evaluating them thoroughly. Background investigations should be done as well as asking many questions to identify proper fit. Reading the required disclosure documents is also highly encouraged. Investors should never rely on someone else to do what they should be doing.

Strategy 2: Seek Out Hedge Fund Managers with Demonstrated Success

Nothing is more important in hedge fund investing than investing with managers that have demonstrated success. Of course, past performance is not a guarantee of future performance, but consistent attractive performance over many years speaks volumes. Performance numbers can be obtained from hedge funds or from an external source. Hedge funds with solid to strong performance will make every effort to communicate to you how well they have done. Conversely, hedge funds with not so attractive performance will not be as forthcoming. One external source for hedge fund information is Morningstar, the same company that was built on providing information and rankings on mutual funds.

Strategy 3: Pursue Hedge Funds with Investor-Friendly Provisions

Although the performance track record of a certain hedge fund is very important, it is not the only factor to take into consideration. Other very important factors that should be evaluated include a high-water mark provision, return hurdle provision, fee structure, and redemption provisions. All else being equal, hedge funds with return hurdles and high-water mark provisions are ideal. At the same time, hedge funds with flexible, instead of stringent, redemption provisions offer investors more opportunities to withdrawal their investment with minimal challenges, or worse yet, headaches. Last, but surely not least, pay attention to hedge fund fee structures. Investigate annual management fees charged against assets under management and performance incentive fees. Ensure that both are not excessive compared to other hedge funds of equal performance and opportunity.

Strategy 4: Evaluate Hedge Funds within the Context of Your Overall Portfolio

Hedge funds should not be viewed as stand-alone investments. Rather, they should be considered within the context of your overall portfolio. That means you understand how your overall portfolio will be impacted when determining how much to invest in hedge funds and what hedge fund strategies to pursue. At the same time, managing the remaining allocations of your portfolio, such as equities, fixed-income and money market instruments, should be accomplished with your hedge fund investments in mind. For example, if you build a portfolio heavily emphasizing equity investments and believe your exposure to equities is excessive given your objectives and constraints, then equity long hedge funds may not be the most appropriate investment. An equity short hedge fund may be more suitable as it will not only limit equity exposure, but also will reduce total equity exposure since the shorts will offset, or neutralize, some of the long positions.

Strategy 5: Diversify Your Hedge Fund Portfolio

Funds of hedge funds provide many benefits that other hedge funds do not. First and foremost, funds of hedge funds provide immediate and enhanced diversification. This is the result of investing in multiple hedge funds and with multiple hedge fund managers. Diversification is ideal as it reduces risk that any one fund or manager will perform poorly and impact your investment. Second, funds of hedge funds provide a means for the investment masses to invest in hedge funds. Most funds of hedge funds have low initial minimums, which is in stark contrast to other types of hedge funds. Other benefits include risk management and professional oversight of where to invest and with whom. The obvious drawback to funds of hedge funds is the second layer of fees charged. Thus investors need to take this into consideration when evaluating this type of fund.

Strategy 6: Switch Hedge Fund Managers When Appropriate

Regardless of the background research you may do, some hedge fund investments simply do not work out. Perhaps the issue is performance related, perhaps the key manager retired, or perhaps the issue is the relationship between the manager and client-investor. Nevertheless, some investors at some point in their investing will find it necessary to walk away and move to another manager. When situations such as this arise, make sure you understand what is expected of you prior to beginning the process of withdrawing your investment. Some hedge funds have flexible provisions for withdrawing investments while others do not. The most important lesson here is to make the switch when the time arises. Waste little time if things are just not working out.

Strategy 7: Be a Rational and Informed Hedge Fund Investor

The number one golden rule of investing is to manage your portfolio as a rational and informed investor. This is smart advice for both hedge fund investing and general investing. If you are able to accomplish this goal then everything else will fall into place.

To become a rational and informed hedge fund investor you will need to be proactive in learning what rational and informed investors do and not do. There are many pitfalls along the way. In addition, you will want to learn the key lessons of hedge funds and investing basics. The final chapter of this book provides a quick and simple discussion of key hedge fund lessons. By knowing the key hedge fund lessons you will position yourself to better manage your portfolio going forward.

What are rational investors? Rational investors do not fall victim to the most common behavioral blunders investors often make. These behavioral blunders include such things as illusion of control, blinders, overconfidence, denial, and herd instinct. By mere definition, rational investors become informed investors over time. Being informed means you know and fully understand key lessons of investing, such as no investment is guaranteed and not to invest in anything you cannot afford to lose. Make a point to become and manage your portfolio as a rational and informed hedge fund investor.

In the next chapter, you will learn about the due diligence activities investors should make to best monitor their hedge funds and their hedge fund managers for continued success.

13

Monitoring Hedge Funds: Due Diligence and Performance Benchmarking After the Initial Investment

Now that we have discussed how best to make the initial hedge fund investment, we turn our attention to what to do after the initial investment is made. Here we will be concentrating our time and efforts on proper due diligence. Monitoring your hedge fund investment thus takes utmost importance. Many people may wonder if monitoring hedge funds is beneficial, let alone possible, given the lack of disclosure made by hedge funds. It is true that many hedge funds will not communicate everything you will want; however, they will communicate enough to help you keep a good handle on how well your hedge fund investment is working out. Monitoring is definitely not one of the more interesting activities of hedge fund investing, but it is one of the most important. There are a few reasons why you should place emphasis on monitoring your hedge fund investment. These reasons include the following:

- Monitoring allows you to keep tabs on the general partner, the person most responsible for your hedge fund performance
- Monitoring allows you to gain a better insight into how your portfolio is being run, what is impacting the performance and what value the hedge fund manager is adding
- Monitoring guards the portfolio against managers making ad hoc decisions that will impede your long-term strategy
- Monitoring allows you to quickly identify performance and ethical issues and to make earlier decisions to resolve these issues
- Monitoring greatly decreases miscommunications and misunderstandings and allows for such occurrences to be quickly and easily resolved
- Monitoring is a form of risk management and control
- Monitoring helps keep the hedge fund manager in tune with your needs
- Monitoring assists the portfolio manager in understanding your objectives and guidelines
- Monitoring ensures that your asset allocation does not stray from the optimal asset allocation

Regardless of how you stay in contact with your hedge fund manager – telephone, email, office visits and social events – staying in contact is very important. Keeping up on the latest happenings in the investment marketplace is another smart move. This is important since you do want to become and remain knowledgeable on the type of investments and markets your hedge fund is invested in. For example, if your hedge fund invests in opportunities presented by global macro events – oil, gold, etc – then keeping up on these is essential. For those investors who want to play a more active role in monitoring their managers and understanding their hedge fund investment, knowing the different strategies available to your manager and how that impacts your portfolio is highly recommended. Monitoring your hedge fund manager is definitely a worthwhile and somewhat complex event. Strive to become an informed and prudent investor capable of making sound investment decisions.

Many hedge fund investors may think that open communication with their hedge fund manager is difficult to achieve. In addition, many may think that hedge fund managers will be cold and unreceptive. This is more fiction than fact. Most hedge fund managers are very approachable and are willing to sit down and talk with you. Before talking with your hedge fund manager, be mindful of the time commitment you require and the number of contacts you make.

Gaining access to your hedge fund manager is much easier when you have a larger portfolio or you are a general partner rather than a limited partner. Given that general partners share in the risk, they are provided with the greatest amount of transparency and disclosure of material information. This of course comes with a price in that general partners have relatively unlimited risk for losses. Limited partners are only liable to the amount of their investment. Furthermore, when you have your own hedge fund account rather than pooling your investment with that of others, you will gain greater access to hedge fund managers. It all boils down to money and influence. The larger your portfolio, the greater access to managers you command.

Potential Areas of Concern

Hedge funds, like traditional investments, have certain areas that have historically exhibited greater areas of concern than others over time. In consequence, your due diligence monitoring warrants a review of the following areas that could impact the performance and success of your hedge fund investment.

Change in Key People

Most hedge funds rely on one or two key people to make all of the hedge fund decisions. These are the very people that have generated solid returns and attracted the attention and interest of their investors. If these key people leave, their talent and skill will leave with them. Filling the vacuum could be an unproven person, or at least unproven with that particular hedge fund. A change in key people commonly triggers investors to follow the key people or simply to seek out another hedge fund altogether.

Decline of Importance

Over time, good hedge funds will gather more assets. The higher the performance, the more assets the fund will gather. When this occurs, hedge funds typically increase their minimum initial investments as the number of available slots for investors gets lower. This means that smaller investors will become overshadowed and thus lose their importance in the eyes of the hedge fund. Some hedge fund managers probably would love to see the small investors leave to open slots for larger investors. Nevertheless, more investors and more assets dilute the influence and importance that any one particular investor holds.

Fraud and Unethical Practices

Nothing can cause an investor to terminate their relationship with a hedge fund and transfer their investment like an incident of fraud or other unethical practice. Trust is so important in hedge fund investing since the disclosure of information is limited. Hedge fund managers command a significant control over their investors' portfolios. Contrary to what the media says about hedge funds, fraud is not widespread. Furthermore, questionable managers can be screened during the hedge fund discovery stage. Exercise caution and keep an eye out for information that appears to be misrepresented or omitted altogether. More severe problems could be lingering as a result.

Prudence Issues

A good hedge fund manager will be placed on a pedestal at some time in their career. Managing hedge funds is a wonderful profession; however, it is also laden with opportunities for managers to become over-confident and gain an ego. This may cause the hedge fund manager to believe he or she can deviate from the existing strategy and try something else. Rational and prudent hedge fund managers recognize this risk and safeguard the portfolio from any such scenarios occurring.

Change in Strategy

A very powerful trend with investing is "the trend is your friend." With hedge funds, this simply means that the investment strategy presently being used is working as needed. Why then would a hedge fund manager change his or her strategy? The primary reason is that the current strategy is not working. Thus, a change in strategy could signal bigger performance issues. In addition, some of the central reasons for investing in certain hedge funds are attributed to the strategy employed. Changing strategies could mean there is no longer a reason to continue investing in the hedge fund.

Ignoring Stated Safeguards and Provisions

Safeguards are put in place to protect the hedge fund and the investor. They also give the hedge fund manager guidelines for how to manage the fund. When these safeguard provisions are ignored, that could mean trouble keeping to the stated plan. Pay particular attention to how the manger is adhering to stated provisions, such as types of instruments used, exposure to asset classes, number of positions permitted, frequency of trading and the size of positions allowed.

Excessive Assets Under Management

Successful hedge funds will attract investors. And this means the assets under management in the hedge fund will grow. Unfortunately, the bigger a fund gets, the more difficult it becomes to manage. The result could be missed opportunities or limited benefit from taking advantage of opportunities. This is because many hedge funds profit from small inefficiencies that must be seized quickly. Consequently, the activity that made the hedge fund successful in the first place cannot be used when the fund becomes successful. Additionally, hedge fund managers may find it necessary to invest in securities with greater risk to make up the difference. Now you have a portfolio with questionable performance opportunities and with more risk. Not the best direction for the fund to head.

Decline in Targeted Investment Opportunities

Over time, the area where a hedge fund targets for investments begins to become less and less opportunistic. The lure of higher returns is too great and that attracts additional interest and competition from other hedge fund managers. Before you know it, returns are lower and the opportunity altogether is gone or at least severely limited. For example, a hedge fund manager invests in a relatively unknown investment in the marketplace, a small growth company. As the company generates strong earnings, the stock price increases and the hedge fund profits. Other hedge funds, always on the lookout for additional opportunities, see this and buy the stock. The original hedge fund will benefit from the new interest in the short-term; however, given the heightened stock valuation, risk has increased and the probability of earning strong returns declines.

Investment Trends Conclude

Some hedge funds rely heavily on certain investment trends. These trends could include movement of interest rates, direction of foreign currency rates, or strength of market sectors. Once these trends decline and finally conclude, the hedge fund is left without an opportunity and the performance of the fund could suffer as a result.

Impact of Leverage

Leveraging the holdings in a hedge fund can be both good and bad. When things are going well, leverage will enhance and magnify the performance. When things are going poorly, leverage will only magnify the loss. At the same time, having leverage leaves the hedge fund susceptible to the decisions of the investment firm granting the loan. When rates tick-up, hedge funds are typically faced with greater interest payments. Increasing the margin requirements is another potential risk to hedge funds employing leverage.

Monitoring Your Hedge Fund Investment

The primary challenge with monitoring hedge funds is transparency, or the ability to investigate a hedge fund and identify its holdings. This is much easier said than done of course. Nevertheless, transparency is key to learning how well the hedge fund is complying with the stated objectives and provisions, such as investment objectives and risk safeguards. Investors deserve to know if the hedge fund is delivering on the stated representations made prior to the initial investment. Not only is this important to individual investors, but also to institutions that ultimately have a fiduciary responsibility to the individual investors they are responsible for investing their money. Lack of disclosure makes the job of monitoring difficult, but not impossible. External sources such as Morningstar can fill the void and provide insights into how well the fund is operating.

Parameter Monitoring

Prior to investing in a hedge fund, an investor will learn a great deal about how the fund is run and what parameters are established and adhered to. A wise investor will from time to time investigate whether or not a hedge fund is following the parameters they initially communicated. Although a lack of transparency will make this challenging, investigating the use of leverage, degree and type of exposure to asset classes, types of instruments used, number of positions held and size of positions held should be done.

Performance Monitoring

Monitoring hedge fund performance is much more complex than comparing the performance to a set benchmark. The primary difficulty arises because hedge funds are commonly invested in many markets and asset classes magnified by the use of leverage and long and short positions. This means that performance results are not entirely comparable with other general benchmarks, such as the S&P 500, the benchmark of choice for traditional investment managers. Benchmarks incorporating returns from peer groups are thus the best solution. Comparing against the S&P 500 is essential, however, as is provides the bogie for justifying hedge fund investing in the first place.

Before beginning your monitoring and evaluation of hedge fund performance, it is a good idea to keep in mind that hedge fund managers are limited by specific capital market related constraints. It is true that hedge fund managers do bring a wealth of skill in profiting from select market opportunities; however, those opportunities do not exist for extended periods of time. By understanding these challenges, investors gain a better grasp of how best to evaluate the performance of a hedge fund manager.

Hedge fund monitoring requires performance comparisons with appropriate benchmarks and related peers. Performance attribution is a key element in succeeding with hedge fund investing. Many hedge fund managers evaluate the performance of a fund or portfolio on a quarterly basis in order to appease the investor. However, evaluating performance is not as easy as it might initially appear. Why? First, there is the issue of evaluating a portfolio's short-term results when you have designed and implemented a long-term strategy. Second, there is difficulty in comparing a multi-asset-class portfolio to a benchmark. Which benchmark or benchmarks do you select? Simply selecting the S&P 500 for a multi-asset-class hedge fund portfolio or fund of hedge funds will not suffice. The S&P 500 is comprised of equity securities only. Thus, a portfolio comprising fixed-income securities or real estate investment trust (REITs) assets simply would not be appropriate. The solution is to segment each asset class and compare it against an appropriate benchmark, such as the S&P 500 for U.S. equity securities and the EAFE for international equity securities.

Lastly, hedge funds should be compared against their primary performance aim – to generate attractive absolute returns. Here you will want to assess how consistent the fund is with generating positive returns. The degree of positive returns is not as important as the consistency of generating those returns. People invest in hedge funds primarily to receive consistent absolute returns. Hedge funds should be judged against this objective.

Risk Management and Control

Monitoring the risk in your portfolio is a wise move, especially for those that do not desire to assume a high degree of risk, or even volatility. Some of the things to look for when monitoring your hedge fund portfolio for risk levels include degree of leverage, use and degree of use of derivative securities, degree of going long or short and finally the underlying risk of the investments targeted given the strategy employed. For example, emerging markets investments will be more risky than strategies pursuing convertible arbitrage. Other factors to consider include investment of public or private securities, degree and type of investment concentration, and adherence to stated objectives and goals. Identifying some of these factors will be challenging as some hedge fund managers will not disclose this information. The best strategy is to work with whatever you have.

Hedge funds are not for the faint of heart. Furthermore, investing in hedge funds is not hassle free, but rather laden with hidden challenges, and opportunities. Regardless of how the situation may be at the beginning, risk management and control is essential given ever changing circumstances. Hedge fund managers change as do their strategies for generating returns. At the same time, investor objectives and constraints change over time. Take risk profile for example. As an investor ages, the need for risk will decline. At the same time, the capacity and perhaps even tolerance will rise. As we know, however, the appropriate risk is the lowest of the three variables. Thus, the portfolio will need to incorporate less risk over time. The monitoring process is definitely not static.

Review and Comparison

Investing in hedge funds can be expensive. With the annual investment management fee and the performance incentive fee, investors need to exercise caution by evaluating performance against other investments, specifically index investments and hedge fund peers. Intuitively, evaluating against peers is just plain common sense. But why then against index investments? Because index investments are your boogie, your true long-term hurdle rate. Since index investments offer the lowest-cost method of diversified investing, measuring a hedge fund against an index can uncover just how much an investor is paying in fees for the difference in performance. There is simply no need to pay extra unless you receive extra performance. If the performance of your hedge fund is not keeping up with the market index, you will want to think long and hard about making a change. The same goes for evaluating your hedge fund against peers. One or two periods of lackluster performance are not necessarily something to worry about, however, more than that and a change should be made. Many people invest in hedge funds for performance reasons so why should anyone stay with hedge funds that cannot deliver? Hedge funds know this as well. Live by the sword, die by the sword.

One final thought about performance measurement and monitoring. It is very important to ensure the performance data is created using geometric returns rather than arithmetic returns. Why? The reason is because the results can be misleading. For instance, your $1,000,000 hedge fund investment suffers a huge loss and is worth $500,000 after one year. That's a negative 50 percent return. The following year your investment gains the $500,000 lost in the previous year giving you a total market value of $1,000,000 at the end of the second year. Thus, you earned a return of 100 percent for year two. Using arithmetic returns, your manager may claim to have earned you a positive 25 percent (–50 percent +100 percent divided by 2) during the two-year period. As you can see, your portfolio has not appreciated whatsoever, thus the +25 percent is not accurate. Using geometric returns, your portfolio manager would report a 0 percent return rather than a +25 percent return. This is something to keep in mind.

Making the Change

As you progress with your monitoring of your hedge fund manager, you may come to a point where a change in managers is warranted. This may be the result of lack of performance, comparably high fees, restrictive provisions for withdrawing invested capital or simply a breakdown in relationship. Nevertheless, making the change is not an especially easy task. Monitoring is a non-stop evaluation of whether or not to hire or fire a hedge fund manager. In general, there is no set rule or provision as to how, where or when to fire your manager. This process is rather subjective but must be approached with an objective mindset to collecting, understanding and balancing the pros and cons.

When the point in time comes where you need to make the change of managers, there are some important factors you should take into consideration. First, the termination process is not the same as other investment relationships given the partnership format. This means that the entire termination process from start to finish could take as long as 90 days. Most take a minimum of 30 days. For audit and paper trails, most hedge fund managers require a written letter from an investor that communicates your request to exit from the partnership. This traditionally occurs and finalizes on fixed periods of time, specifically calendar quarters. The offering memorandum and other disclosure documents will outline in writing everything that an investor must do to exit from the partnership. Some even charge you a redemption fee upon leaving to cover costs and as a deterrent to leaving. Although they will not say it is for that purpose.

Upon leaving, some managers will give you cash while others will give you securities in lieu of cash. Receiving securities has its drawbacks. First, securities may have embedded capital gains that otherwise should have been sold in the fund and spread out amount the entire group of investors, not just one. Second, securities may be relatively illiquid and thus difficult to sell at the stated market value.

Although the process is difficult at best, most hedge fund managers are sensible people who will sit down with you and try to work out the issue. If no resolution can be found, the hedge fund manager will help to facilitate the termination and transfer of assets. Many investors terminating their relationship will discover the process resembles that of traditional investment portfolio terminations. In this case, however, the investor may want to take the lead role in identifying how best to transfer the securities. Some may want to transfer the entire lot while others may only want to transfer some securities with the rest transferred in cash. Investors who find themselves in this situation will want to take the lead role as hedge fund managers may not have the best interest of the terminating investor at heart.

Fund of Hedge Funds Consideration

Funds of hedge funds are growing steadily in popularity. One of the primary reasons for this growth is the professional management and oversight of other hedge funds. This means that an experienced investment professional is reviewing and evaluating other hedge funds for hiring and firing purposes. Thus, the monitoring process that many investors will typically do is not managed by a professional. However, this does not excuse the investor from his or her responsibility of reviewing the hedge fund for performance, fees, taxes, risks, fit and other factors related to due diligence. The best person for looking after your interests is you. Managers of fund of hedge funds do a superb job in evaluating performance, talking with hedge fund managers and making good decisions for the hedge fund, but that does not mean investors can outsource this role.

Performance Benchmarking

With traditional investing, measuring performance against a specific index or benchmark is necessary to ascertain how well the portfolio has performed. This of course is relative performance benchmarking. Absolute performance benchmarking does not require an index per se since you only need to generate a positive return to accomplish the aim of absolute performance. The same is not true of relative performance. With relative performance, a benchmark is selected that accurately reflects the investments in the portfolio or fund you will use to compare. For example, the most widely used performance benchmark with traditional investing is the S&P 500. That is because many of the stocks in the S&P 500 are held in traditional investment portfolios or companies very similar, but not represented in the index. This means that comparing against this index is the most appropriate approach.

Until recently, the challenge of hedge fund investing was the lack of appropriate indices to benchmark performance. This has changed recently as more and more sources are establishing indices to track either one particular hedge fund strategy or the entire field in aggregate. The very first basic indices appeared in the 1980s, but they were not widely followed.

In 2004, *the Wall Street Journal* began publishing several hedge fund indices to enable readers to make quick and easy relative comparisons. Investors are thus better informed as to how well or poorly their funds have done compared to others. Other indices have also been established for the same reasons. You will also find that some of the indices are established by hedge fund managers simply to get their name out in the hedge fund investing marketplace. Nevertheless, the following page lists some of the more well-known hedge fund indices.

Some of the indices, due to construction flaws, have built-in biases and inconsistencies. However, they do provide a nice way for investors to gauge the direction of hedge fund performance and by how much. Over time, the hedge fund industry will move to one or more primary indices

INDICES	INCEPTION	NUMBER OF STRATEGY INDICES	WEIGHTING METHODOLOGY
Standard & Poor's Indices	2002	10	Simple Mean
HFR	1994	37	Simple Mean
Dow Jones	2003	5	NAV Calculation
Altvest	2000	14	Simple Mean
CSFB/Tremont	1999	14	Asset Weighted Mean
MSCI Indices	2002	4	Asset Weighted Mean & Simple Mean
Van Edge	1994	25	Simple Mean
Hennessee	1987	24	Simple Mean

Figure 13-1   Hedge Fund Indices

for evaluating performance, much like what traditional investing has done. This may involve the S&P Hedge Fund Index due to name and investor confidence, or not. Only time will tell.

Investable Indices

There are essentially two forms of investing – active management and passive management. Hedge fund investing is predominately active management while index funds and exchange-traded funds represent an approach to passive investing. Holding an S&P 500 index fund is passive investing at its fundamental level. There are many index funds available for investors to hold in their portfolio. With hedge fund investing, investing in indices is not as easy. There are only a couple of indices available for investors to buy to gain returns comparable to the hedge fund strategy the index tracks. Three of the more popular indices include the S&P Hedge Fund Index, Financial Times Stock Exchange, and MSCI (Morgan Stanly Capital International). Each of these strategies attempts to track and deliver a return that mirrors the return of the aggregate hedge fund market. In the future we will most definitely see more investable indices hit the marketplace. In addition, I would not be surprised to see passive traditional exchange-traded funds established to track any number of hedge fund strategies.

Drawbacks with Hedge Fund Indices

Most of the hedge fund indices are created using information collected on a monthly basis involving performance numbers from thousands of hedge funds. These performance numbers are collected and entered using either analyst entry or manager entry. Altvest and HedgeFund.net employ the manager entry method while the rest of the commercial databases employ the analyst entry, according to a study entitled "A Comparison of Major Hedge Fund Data Sources" conducted by software company Strategic Financial Solutions. This study also found errors in the data assembled by the data sources, such as fee requirements, performance, required minimum investment, and hedge fund strategy employed. Nevertheless, the information provided by these data sources is more beneficial than not.

One of the big reasons for the discrepancy of information stems from the inconsistency of hedge fund managers in reporting to hedge fund databases. Some managers do not provide data while others pick and chose to whom they will report data. This creates issues among indices. In addition to the inconsistent reporting, hedge fund managers sometimes will not report numbers if performance is poor. This means that performance could be biased to the high side as offsetting poor returns are omitted. Lastly, if a hedge fund were to close, some data sources do not account for this and simply continue to report on the existing funds. When benchmarks only reflect existing funds and not closed funds, then these indices are said to have survivorship bias. This means that performance numbers are distorted and higher than they should be under actual conditions. The performance of closed funds should be included in historical performance.

Another issue with hedge fund indices relates to the classification of hedge fund strategy. One company may classify all hedge fund strategies in ten distinct groups while another company may classify all hedge fund strategies in fifteen distinct groups. Thus, there is confusion with investors as to which index is best for benchmarking purposes. Over time I suspect we will see more accepted categories and thus standardized hedge fund indices.

Benchmarking Summary

Even with the aforementioned issues with hedge fund indices, they provide more than adequate means for investors to benchmark the performance of their hedge fund investment as compared to the hedge fund industry. This benchmarking will give investors better knowledge of how well their manager is doing and whether or not to move their investment to another hedge fund manager. In the not so distant future hedge fund indices will become significantly more standardized and thus even more valuable to hedge fund investors.

In the next chapter, you will learn about techniques and tactics investors can employ to bypass hedge fund managers and manage their portfolio like hedge funds.

PART FOUR

FINAL THOUGHTS ON WHAT YOU NEED TO KNOW

14

Self-Manage Strategy: Trading Techniques to Manage Your Portfolio Like a Hedge Fund

In certain circumstances it may be more appropriate to forgo investing in hedge funds and instead manage your existing portfolio in the same manner as a hedge fund manager might. Perhaps an investor does not find the liquidity provisions ideal or does not want to make the financial commitment necessary to invest in a particular hedge fund. The reasons for bypassing hedge funds can be numerous, including the simple desire and passion to manage your own portfolio and overcome the related challenges. Nevertheless, employing one of the techniques presented in this chapter may help to create a trading fund much like that of hedge fund managers.

As you can imagine, these trading techniques are not overly complex, nor difficult to understand. Rather, they are more simple and straight-forward than most common practices of hedge fund managers. These trading techniques should not be considered conservative nor have inherent low volatility. They are generally considered high risk and should be evaluated within this context before embarking on a plan to employ these trading techniques.

Trade Spread Arbitrages

Under this trading technique, an investor will want to go long one security and go short a second security that is highly correlated. The investor will need to do research on the historical trading spreads between two like securities and identify a normal trading spread. If this spread were to become too narrow or too wide due to any number of factors, then an investor can take advantage of this opportunity by shorting the security that has not lost value and go long the security that has seen the most value decline. The expectation is that the spread will revert to the normal range, thus generating profits.

> EXAMPLE: An investor is scouring the newspapers and reads about company A not doing so well. As a result, the investor identifies a strong price relationship over the past several years with company B. The price decline in company A stock has widened the spread between it and company B. The investor sees this opportunity and buys the stock of company A and sells short the stock of company B. Once, or if, the spread were to revert back to normal spreads, then the investor will gain on the price appreciation of the long position and could gain on a price decline on the short position.

Trade Securities Facing Index Removal

There are numerous indices in the United States that track a certain and specific area of the market. We have index funds that track the S&P 500, NASDAQ, Wilshire, Dow Jones Industrials, Russell Indexes, S&P 500 value stocks, and even indices tracking commodities, real estate, and hedge funds. Given the incredible explosion of index funds and exchange-traded funds over the last several years, the amount of assets these indices hold is truly astounding. This means that they influence, albeit indirectly, the price of the securities comprising the indices.

From time to time, the powers to be will make changes in each index in an effort to effectively reflect the market segment they are attempting to capture. This involves removing a security and including another security. When this happens, there is a lag between the time the announcement is made and the time when the security switch is made. When the day comes that the exchange is made, institutions that run the index funds will sell the security that has been removed and buy the security that has been added. This creates artificial supply and demand for the two particular securities involved. For investors, this opens up two trading opportunities that can be accomplished after the announcement, but before the exchange is made. These two include the following:

* To short the security that is being removed
* To buy the security that is being added

A research study entitled "Investor Awareness and Market Segmentation: Evidence from S&P 500 Changes", conducted by Honghui Chen of the University of Baltimore, Gregory Noronha of Arizona State University West, and Vijay Singal of Virginia Tech, concluded that stocks typically rise about 5 percent during the period between the announcement of the exchange and the date of the actual exchange. They also concluded that stocks removed from the index did not decline in price as much as they gained. As a result, investors may have opportunities to capture profits from this occurrence.

Trade Securities Facing Opportunistic Credit Rating Changes

Many institutions are not permitted to own fixed-income securities that have below investment grade credit ratings. Many can only own those with investment grade ratings, generally considered ratings of BBB- or higher. This means that institutions create artificial supply and demand without any other regard simply as a matter of policy. Consequently, investors might be able to profit from this situation by selling short securities that institutions will be forced to sell and purchasing securities that institutions will be able to buy at some time in the near future.

Credit rating agencies – Fitch, Standard & Poors and Moody's – often publish credit watch announcements or communicate which direction they believe the financials of a certain company are heading. Thus, if Moody's believes a cut in a certain company's fixed-income rating is on the horizon, this could signal an opportunity for an investor to sell short the investment. Then, if the credit rating is cut by Moody's to non-investment grade, institutions will be forced to liquidate their holdings, thus driving down the price in the process. Someone with a short position would benefit from this move.

Likewise, a bond that is on credit watch to be upgraded from non-investment grade to investment grade is a prime candidate for purchase as an upgrade to investment grade will create extra buying demand. Note that credit rating upgrades and downgrades themselves influence prices as well.

Trade Based on Option Expiration Day

One day per month the financial markets have what is called option expiration day, or OED for short. On this day, the market is very active with opportunities to take advantage of price inefficiencies and price trends. Many investment gurus have come out with different ways to profit around this day, with many working and many not. The best scenario is where an investor makes a small profit. The chances of doing just this are typically less than two in three. However, since there are twelve months in the year, investors have twelve opportunities to trade around OED. Some of the more well-known trades that offer reasonable chances of success, meaning more chances to profit than to lose, include the following:

- Purchase S&P 500 Index Funds on options expiration and hold for one week, plus or minus one day. Results are generally favorable.
- Sell short the NASDAQ 100 (QQQQ) the day prior to the option expiration day close. Then turn around and sell the security the following day on option expiration day. Historical returns show decent returns from this trade.

Trade Bankrupt Securities

This trading technique involves purchasing a security that has recently announced that it has filed for bankruptcy. This is not to be confused with rumors floating around that a certain company will declare bankruptcy in the near future. No, this is the real actual deal. Under this technique, an investor will purchase the stock of a company that has filed for bankruptcy once the stock exchange has reopened trading given the halt in stock trading from the announcement. One can attribute the abnormal gain in stock price after a bankruptcy has been filed to the hordes of people that were fully anticipating this event and oversold the stock simply to get out. Oversold conditions are ripe for generating short-term profits when the right conditions are present. Aside from oversold conditions driving stock prices higher after a bankruptcy announcement, investors may get a new sense of interest in the security since the company will mostly likely become healthier financially without burdensome debt levels.

EXAMPLE: An investor is listening to CNBC when he hears about Company DD filing for bankruptcy protection that very day. The investor checks the stock price and discovers that the price has declined to $0.75 per share, but the trading is halted for release of the bankruptcy news to be disseminated. The investor believes that former shareholders were forecasting this scenario and sold their stock thus creating an oversold opportunity. Once the exchange reopens trading for Company DD, the investor purchases shares of the company with the hope that the price will rise over the short-term. The investor's downside is the cost of the investment and the gain could be substantially more than the original investment.

Trade Securities Close to the End of Time Periods

There are certain times during the year when investors, both institutional and individual, tend to make transactions. For example, December is a popular month for making tax-loss sales while January is a popular month for reinvesting the proceeds of the tax-loss sales. Quarter ends also provide opportunities for investors as money managers sometimes engage in what is called window-dressing, or buying and selling securities all with the aim of making their holdings look attractive to prospective investors since many money managers report holdings on a quarterly basis. The beginning of the new year is also a time when certain investment managers implement their strategies. The Dogs of the Dow strategy is a prime example. Under this strategy, a manager will invest the pool of funds into the ten highest yielding stocks in the Dow Jones Industrial Average. Each year the portfolio is rebalanced to accommodate only those ten highest yielding stocks. As an investor, knowing which Dow Jones stock will be sold and purchased in masses could generate an edge.

Investors might be able to better manage their purchases and sales by taking these aforementioned actions into consideration. For instance, if an investor wants to sell a certain security and purchase another, perhaps that investor could sell in November prior to the bulk of tax-loss selling and purchase one of the ten highest yielding Dow Jones stocks that is currently not in that list and thus will be included. This timing of purchases and sales may not provide a material gain, but even little gains can add up.

Trade Securities with a Short Bias

Under this trading technique, investors will search for securities they believe are overvalued. These securities can be equities, fixed-income, commodities, or real estate. Exchange-traded funds provide a good way to invest in the alternative markets.

The aim of the investor is to sell short the securities at a high price and to buy them back at a much lower price. What is nice about this trading technique is that investors can find securities in practically any market regardless of whether prices are advancing or falling. Purchasing an equity index fund to offset the impact of the market can also be incorporated into this trading technique. The side benefit to this trading technique is the receipt of the short interest rebate. When securities are sold short, the proceeds of the sale are generally held at the brokerage firm where they earn interest like any other money market account.

The risk of course to this trading technique is that the overvalued security continues to move higher in price rather than decline in price. Once a security is sold short, losses mount if the security rises in value. Theoretically, investors who sell short have unlimited loss potential as the price of the security sold short has the possibility of continuing to move higher. Risk is limited to the invested capital on long positions since prices can only go to zero. This assumes no leverage.

Trade Hedge Funds as a Fund of Hedge Funds

For those investors with a good deal of time, patience, and assets, managing their portfolio like a fund of hedge funds could be a wise move. Why pay the extra layer of fees for a fund of hedge funds manager if you do not have to do so? This is obviously not a trading technique for those with little time or patience. A good deal of research on the different hedge fund options will need to be conducted as well as face to face interviews. Another hurdle to this trading technique is the level of wealth an investor may need. Investing in one or two hedge funds will require a significant amount of invested capital so any more than two could make this trading technique not feasible.

The advantage of this trading technique is not only more control over which hedge fund managers manage an investor's wealth, but also the elimination of the second layer of fees typically charged by funds of hedge funds. These fees generally run around 1 to 2 percent for asset-based fees and 10 to 12 percent for performance incentive fees.

Trade to Create Equity Market Neutral

Many hedge fund managers employ this very strategy to manager their hedge funds. Investors can do the same thing. Since this trading technique essentially removes the risk of the market, security-specific risk is thus magnified and an important consideration when making investment decisions. Investors should only use this trading technique when they are confident in their abilities to pick winning securities.

Under this trading technique, an investor will purchase a security they believe will appreciate in value and generate attractive returns. Focusing on security-specific factors and return potential should be emphasized. About the same time the security is purchased, an equity index fund is sold short to reduce or eliminate altogether the risk associated with the overall market. I use the word reduce as a less than perfect price correlation will leave some open exposure to market risk. Selling short an S&P 500 Index Fund is a popular choice, but investors should target those equity indices that best represent the security purchased. Why is market risk reduced or eliminated? When an investor holds a security, that security is exposed to risk from the market and is influenced by market prices. By selling short an index fund, the movement of the security from market factors will be offset by the movement in the index fund. Both will rise or decline in price together, but when the long is losing value the short will be gaining in value and vice versa.

The end result will be a portfolio with a long position in an individual security and a short position in an equity index fund. Only security specific risk remains. This same trading technique can be used for fixed-income securities as well, although finding an index is very challenging. Thus, replacing the market index fund with another fixed-income security can be accomplished.

Trade Around Merger Opportunities

One good trading technique investors can quickly and easily implement is a merger arbitrage trading technique. Under this trading technique, an investor will invest in the stock of two companies involved in a merger deal. With nearly all merger or acquisition deals, there is a spread between the acquisition price and the current market price of the company being acquired. This spread is the market's signal of how confident they are in the deal going through to completion. Large spreads indicate low confidence from the market while small spreads indicate high confidence that all will go well.

To best take advantage of merger deals and make a profit, an investor will want to go long the company that is being acquired and sell short the company that is doing the acquisition. The aim of this strategy is to profit on the narrowing or elimination of the spread once the two companies complete the merger. For example, if a company is being acquired for $75 a share and the current market price of that company is $74, then the profit potential is $1. Once the deal is complete, the shareholders will receive $75 in cash or stock in the company making the acquisition. Thus, investors will have earned their $1 profit. The proceeds from the stock sold short can be used to fund the purchase of the stock of the company being acquired.

The risk with this trading technique is that the deal does not go to fruition and the investor is stuck with a stock that will revert to pre-merger price levels, or somewhat higher. This could mean a large loss for the investor. Caution must thus be exercised.

Trade using a Macro-Centric Viewpoint

Macro-centric hedge funds are some of the most widely used and popular hedge funds around today. Under this strategy, an investor will make directional price bets on more macro investments and bypass specific investments. For instance, an investor may target investments in Europe or Asia. Other possibilities include investments in foreign exchange rates or commodity prices. This trading technique is considered a "top-down" approach to hedge fund investing.

Individual investors may find index funds the best solution to investing in the macro markets as they provide instant diversification, availability, and low cost. There are numerous index funds and exchange-traded funds (ETFs) available for investors. One good source for information on ETFs is iShares.com.

Trade using a Multi-Strategy Approach

Instead of investors using one particular trading technique, they may want to consider following the multi-strategy approach that many hedge fund managers employ. Under this strategy, an investor will use two or more trading strategies to manage his or her portfolio like a hedge fund. For instance, the investor could employ merger arbitrage trading and equity market neutral strategies. Some trading strategies do not go together as well as other strategies do, but the use of multiple strategies could deliver the diversification an investor may want.

In the next chapter, you will learn about hedge funds under the microscope by exploring the ten defining characteristics of hedge funds.

15

Top Ten Defining Characteristics: Hedge Funds Under the Microscope

Now that we have explored all of the major topics of hedge funds, we turn our attention to zeroing in on exactly what are the defining characteristics of hedge funds. This chapter will present what, in my judgment, are the top ten defining characteristics of hedge funds. Each of these defining characteristics was discussed at length in this book, but now we bring each of them together in one chapter to reinforce their importance with hedge funds.

If there is anything that you take away from this book, understanding and remembering the top ten defining characteristics is the best approach. These defining characteristics are presented in no particular order and no one defining characteristic is any more important than another.

Figure 15-1   Top 10 Defining Characteristics of Hedge Funds

1. Unique Structure and Organization

Hedge funds are quite different from other investment organizations, including mutual funds. Hedge funds are typically established as limited liability companies or limited partnerships. Sometimes hedge funds are established where the general partner, or the person with unlimited liability, is actually a limited liability company. Hedge funds also differ slightly in where the fund is domiciled – either domestically as an onshore hedge fund or in a hedge fund haven as an offshore hedge fund. Other forms include commodity pools and separately managed accounts. Each has its own benefits and merits for using.

Hedge funds ascribe to the small is better philosophy. As such, hedge funds are typically much smaller in size, scope, and key people. Most hedge funds are run by one or two key people rather than an investment committee such as with mutual funds. Smaller can be both good and bad. The bad reason is that the margin for error is exceptionally smaller given fewer people to make important decisions. The good reason is that having fewer decision makers lends itself to making faster decisions and taking advantage of investment opportunities very quickly. Many hedge fund companies are dominated by one or two key people.

Another drawback of having a smaller investment company is that they will typically have fewer assets given the lack of framework to handle more investors. Restrictions on the type and number of clients will cause even greater problems.

Lastly, hedge fund managers commonly do something that most other investment managers do not do – invest a substantial amount of their own personal assets into the fund. This is frequently done to give the client confidence in knowing that the hedge fund manger believes in the story and invests in it.

2. Minimal Oversight & Regulation

The hedge fund industry is regulated on many fronts. However, in aggregate, hedge funds are far less regulated than are mutual funds and other traditional investments. Unlike mutual funds, hedge funds are not required to provide daily liquidity to their investors nor must they disclose the same level of information that mutual funds are required to disclose. This minimal oversight and regulation allows hedge fund managers to stretch their arms and employ investment strategies that more traditional managers are not permitted to employ.

Some the of the major players involved in regulating some aspect of hedge funds include the Securities and Exchange Commission (SEC), Commodity Futures Trading Commission (CFTC), Federal Reserve, United States Treasury, and are indirectly regulated by banks, brokerage firms, and the National Association of Securities Dealers (NASD) via their business relationships with hedge funds.

The most important regulations impacting hedge funds include, but are not limited to, the Investment Company Act of 1940, Investment Advisers Act of 1940, anti-fraud laws, insider trading laws, and the Commodity Exchange Act.

3. Restricted to a Low Number of "Accredited Investors"

Hedge funds are severely restricted by the number and types of investors they are allowed to accept. This restriction is placed on hedge funds by the SEC as a trade-off for the freedom of employing nearly any investment tool desired. The SEC only permits hedge funds to accept investors that fit the definition of "accredited investor." To quality for this definition, investors must pass some basic net worth hurdles, such as having earned at least $200,000 annually in income for the past two years – and have a reasonable expectation of doing so into the future – and having a net worth of at least $1 million after excluding personal residences and automobiles. In addition, hedge funds are restricted to a limited and low number of investors. Compounding the situation for hedge funds are the restrictions on marketing and promotion. Thus, hedge funds have to exercise more effort to find suitable investors for their funds.

4. Restrictive Liquidity and Redemption Provisions

Unlike mutual funds and other traditional investments, hedge funds for the most part have restrictive liquidity and redemption provisions. With mutual funds, if an investor wants to withdraw their investments, they only need to call their fund company and request a redemption. Days later a check will show up in the mail. In addition, shareholders in mutual funds can determine the price and value of their investment on any given day since mutual funds provide such information daily. The SEC requires mutual funds not only to provide daily liquidity, but also to provide daily pricing. The same is not true for hedge funds.

Hedge funds do not provide daily valuations or monthly valuations. Furthermore, hedge funds have tough restrictions on withdrawing or redeeming investments. Most hedge funds have what is called a "lock-up period" for new investors. This means that new investors are not permitted to withdraw their invested capital for a certain predetermined period, typically one year after the initial investment is made. This is implemented to protect the hedge fund manager from making otherwise long-term investments with the new money and then being forced to sell after only a brief time to accommodate a request for funds.

In addition to a lock-up provision, hedge funds commonly only permit the withdrawal of funds at certain times during the year. This is typically done on a quarterly basis. Some permit monthly withdrawals while others opt for longer periods of one year. Once a new investor passes the lock-up period, they then must follow the standard redemption provisions of all hedge fund investors. These provisions are spelled out in the offering material hedge funds provide to interested parties prior to making the initial investment

5. Limitations on Marketing and Promotions

The United States Securities and Exchange Commission places strict regulations and limitations on how and to whom hedge funds can market their hedge fund offerings. Since the SEC is out to protect the general investing public, they want to minimize any contact and investment possibilities with investors that are not qualified to invest in any given hedge fund. The complexity of hedge funds and their transactions will also make this more challenging.

Hedge funds are restricted from airing radio or television commercials since the general investing public may be exposed to the message and investigate making an investment, and the SEC has provided restrictions on the type of person hedge funds can market and promote. Why then would hedge funds use radio to market their funds so people who do not qualify will hear the message and seek to invest. It doesn't make any sense. Also removed from the publicity arsenal for hedge fund managers are print advertising or any other medium where the general investing public will hear.

6. Extensive Tools of the Trade

Perhaps there is no more significant difference between traditional investing and alternative investing, including hedge funds, than in their tools of the trade. More specifically, in the tactics and techniques hedge fund managers employ to manage their funds. These tools include using leverage, selling short, trading derivatives, investing in deeply discounted securities or overly valued securities, and pursuing arbitrage opportunities.

Traditional investment managers are for all intensive purposes restricted from using these tools. This is attributed to safeguards implemented by the SEC and forced on managers if they wish to deal with the general investing public. The SEC believes these tools increase risk, and they can. Therefore the SEC places hand-cuffs on managers if they want to invest money for investors who lack the knowledge and experience in dealing with these tools.

In contrast, hedge funds use these tools extensively to take advantage of opportunities and make the best of certain special situations. These tools provide the hedge fund managers with substantially greater flexibility and alternatives than the mutual fund manager or other traditional managers. The simple ability to sell short provides the hedge fund manager with the opportunity to offset risk associated with the market or certain sectors. In addition, funds can be developed that can generate profits in any market, regardless of overall market declines or market advances. Another important tool hedge fund managers use is that of leverage. Leverage allows the hedge fund manager to magnify the performance. Leverage is essentially borrowing capital from a brokerage firm or bank and then using that capital to buy more of a specific asset. As long as the return of the invested asset is greater than the borrowing cost then the hedge fund will have made a smart move and enhanced performance. The remaining tools are all used by different hedge fund managers at different times. Most hedge fund managers stick with one or two tools and emphasize only those. They do not use all the tools available to them at any one point. This would create a jack of all trades and master of none.

7. Absolute Returns

In the world of investing, most pooled funds seek good relative perfor-mance. Relative performance is essentially performing well against the peer group. Regardless of how well or poorly a mutual fund manager has performed, the real comparison is with how well or poorly the rest of the peer group performed. Hedge funds, on the other side of the pendulum, seek good absolute performance. Absolute performance and relative per-formance are not the same. With absolute performance, a hedge fund manager strives to generate positive returns, not knock the cover off the ball returns. Hedge funds are all about reducing risk and enhancing return smartly. Absolute performance is aligned with this aim.

Many people think hedge funds are a means of reducing risk. This is an excusable consideration given the name and history of hedge funds. Unfortunately, most hedge funds do not reduce total risk. Many actually create additional risk. Specifically speaking, hedge funds seek strong per-formance. This means attractive historical returns, low dispersion of historical returns, and high consistencies of historical returns.

The benefits of absolute returns include experiencing a positive return and holding an asset class that exhibits low volatility. Low volatility is the result of the pursuit of absolute returns, not the objective per se. When returns are fluctuating all over the place, fund volatility will be high. And as we know, higher volatility means higher risk. Hedge funds do not have these same big swings in value given the strategies they employ to generate absolute returns, or positive returns in any investment market.

Lastly, hedge funds and mutual funds have different sources of return and risk. The source of risk and return for mutual funds is market timing, strategy employed by the manager, and the care and skill of the manager to implement, monitor, and manage the strategy to take advan-tage of profitable opportunities. Given the ability and willingness of hedge funds to short securities, market risk can be minimized to a fair degree. As a result, hedge funds face only investment strategy risk and the risk associated with how the strategy is implemented.

8. Ideally Low Correlations

Hedge fund managers can employ many different tactics and techniques to manage their funds. As a result of their use of these tools, hedge funds exhibit low correlations with the equity markets and other asset classes. Correlation is a measurement of how closely the market prices of two assets move together over time. Thus, high correlation means that the prices of two assets are changing and moving in very similar ways and patterns. On the flip side, low correlations mean that the prices of the two assets are moving differently from one another. The lower the correlation the less the prices move together. Low correlation could mean they still move in roughly the same direction or even totally opposite directions.

Holding a portfolio of assets with low correlations to other assets is ideal since when one asset is moving down in price, another will not fall as much or even will rise in value. Hedge funds have low correlations and thus move differently from the market, specially the equity markets. Although the assets held in hedge funds do play a role in determining fund correlation, it is the tactics and techniques that really drive low correlations. Since hedge fund managers have the ability to sell short, the reverse correlation is thus incorporated. For example, if two stocks have a high correlation close to +1, which means they move in perfect lock-step form, then selling short one of those stocks will create correlation that is close to –1, which means they move in perfect opposite lock-step form. Note that the correlation of the two stocks will continue to have high positive correlation, but the effect of the sell short will deliver negative correlation to the fund

To enable hedge fund managers to deliver on their aim of absolute returns, holding low correlation assets is essential to counter the movement in the equity markets. Thus, when the market is declining, a low correlation fund may still deliver gains.

9. Dynamic Fee Arrangement

Hedge funds charge two types of fees. The first is the standard investment management fee and the second is the performance incentive fee. Nearly all traditional investment funds charge the standard investment management fee, typically around 1 percent. This figure could be slightly more or slightly less. Hedge funds generally charge the same fee. This fee covers the expenses of the fund – mutual or hedge. The second fee is what differentiates hedge funds altogether, the performance incentive fee. This fee is charged against the profits generated by the hedge fund. The typical performance incentive fee is 20 percent, with some higher and some lower, and is assessed annually based on the performance of the previous year. If the fund does not generate a positive return and make money for the investor, then the fee is not charged. Furthermore, certain safeguards are oftentimes used to protect the investor from paying twice or even more on gains the fund had earned in the past, but lost in subsequent years. Please see the following defining characteristic for more on these safeguards.

Some people may become uncomfortable when they hear that hedge funds can charge 20 percent fees on profits generated. The point to remember is that hedge funds earn this fee, or at least better be, by delivering on their aim of absolute returns, or consistent positive returns even when the equity market is declining. It's better to pay a 20 percent fee on a 10 percent annual return than a zero percent fee on a –5 percent annual return. Many hedge funds earn their keep.

10. High-Water Mark and Hurdle Rate Safeguards

Given the high fees that hedge funds charge investors in the form of a performance incentive fee, safeguards are typically implemented to protect the investor. The two safeguards most prevalent with hedge funds include the high-water mark and the hurdle rate. Most hedge funds have the high-water mark, but few have the hurdle rate safeguard.

The high-water mark is a safeguard established to protect the investor from paying the performance incentive fee on the exact same gains. The high-water mark is the point where all gains above this level are charged the fee. Thus, if a $1 million portfolio loses $100,000 in one year and the next gains $200,000, then the performance incentive fee is only charged on $100,000 since the other $100,000 only got the portfolio back to the original starting point, or in this case the high-water mark. Given the gain, the new high-water mark moves to $1.1 million and only gains above that amount are charged to the client.

The hurdle rate basically says that only gains above a certain rate will be charged the performance incentive fee. Most hurdle rates are tied to LIBOR (London Interbank Offering Rate) or the rate on Treasury bills. Funds that implement hurdle rate safeguards will typically still implement the high-water mark. In a certain year if the LIBOR rate was 4.5 percent, then only gains associated with returns above the 4.5 percent are charged the fee. Thus, if a certain portfolio generated a return of 5 percent, then only gains from 0.5 percent will incur the performance incentive fee.

In the next chapter, you will learn about the future of hedge funds and the areas where hedge funds will most likely experience the greatest change from today's investing landscape.

16

Future of Hedge Funds: Perspectives, Outlook, and Developing Trends

Hedge funds have become a significant force with investing and wealth management. The growth of the trade is truly astounding. Today, there are close to 9000 hedge funds with well over $1 trillion in assets under management. The market of the recent couple of decades provided the foundation and support for hedge funds to grow and flourish with the conditions ripe for an industry with strong potential and interest. However, let's put the past behind us for a moment and think about the future and what it may hold for hedge fund investing. Many questions quickly surface when we think about this topic. Will present-day conditions continue into the future or will they disappear? Will government regulations squeeze the industry, essentially turning hedge funds into glorified mutual funds or will they continue to provide little regulation? One thing is for certain, the hedge fund trade will experience changes over the foreseeable future. But what will these changes specifically impact? Figure 16-1

Figure 16-1   Ten Probable Changes to the Hedge Fund Trade

illustrates the ten changes, in my judgment, will occur in the future to the hedge fund trade.

1. Hedge Fund Companies will Increase in Size and Offerings

This trend has been developing for some time now as existing hedge fund companies expand in size, scope, and establish new hedge funds in their product offerings. Over the next few years, hedge fund companies will strive to add more funds and grow their companies, thus capturing economies of scale. With the money many of these hedge funds earn, funding more expansion will not be especially difficult. This expansion will most likely create mega-hedge fund companies that offer hedge funds in each strategy with multi-strategies and fund of hedge funds offerings included to enhance and complete what they offer to institutional and high-net worth investors. A push to become more consultative will also occur over the next several years.

2. Hedge Fund Regulation will Rise

This is another trend that has been ongoing for some time and is fully expected to continue into the foreseeable future. Without a doubt, the SEC will hunt for ways to regulate hedge funds. We have seen this in practically everything they do and say regarding hedge funds. The end result of this heightened regulation will most likely include the following:

- Full registration of hedge fund managers
- Greater disclosure of hedge fund assets and holdings
- Modest limitations on tactics and techniques used by hedge fund managers
- Increased liquidity
- More stringent regulations on who is an "accredited investor"

Entities that will bring their influence – both positive and negative – to bear on the hedge fund trade include governmental regulatory entities, related third parties such as broker dealers and institutional investors, and political entities. It is only a matter of time before regulatory entities sink their teeth into hedge funds.

3. Reduced Hedge Fund Fees

The question is not if, but when hedge fund fees will decline overall. Asset-based fees are most likely to remain largely intact and untouched; however, performance incentive fees will see pressure due to two primary factors. First, with so many new hedge funds being established, managers will reduce their rates from the common 20 percent level of profits to give them an advantage over other managers. This will set them apart and attract additional investors. Second, with many institutional investors increasing their allocations to hedge funds, pressure to reduce rates will increase. These institutions will trade capital invested for a reduced rate; a quantity discount of sorts. Many managers will continue to keep their 20-1 (performance incentive and asset-based) fees steady given strong historical performance and resulting demand for their services. However, for the most part, hedge fund managers will experience declines in the fees they charge, much like what mutual funds experienced many years ago.

4. Enhanced Hedge Fund Indices

Index-based investing is not a new approach to traditional investing, but is new with hedge fund investing. Over time, more standardized investable indices will emerge that will enable investors to generate returns that mirror the performance of any one of the different hedge fund strategies. Soon hedge fund investors will be able to hold index-based derivatives, now in its infancy. In addition, hedge fund indices themselves will improve as there is a concerted effort by data providers and hedge fund managers to provide the best data possible to construct accepted indices. Given the pressure from institutions to provide greater transparency, hedge fund managers will improve their data provided to not only their institutional investors, but also to those that construct indices. This means that both institutional and retail investors will have better and more reliable benchmarks to facilitate performance measurement and on-going investment decisions.

5. Enhanced Investor Liquidity

Most hedge funds impose one year lock-up periods for new money and 90 days notification periods before withdrawing money from existing investments. For hedge funds that invest in long-term investments such as venture capital projects or highly illiquid assets, requiring long periods of time before withdrawing money is more than fair and appropriate. However, much of the remaining investments held in a hedge fund can be liquidated in a relatively short period of time, such as weeks or even days. This means that hedge fund managers have the flexibility to change their requirements and thus enhance investor liquidity. In doing so, hedge fund managers will set themselves apart from other managers and that will help them attract additional investments from both institutional and high-net worth investors. Many hedge fund managers will move to enhanced investor liquidity on their own, while others will be either highly motivated or required to do so by institutional investors and governmental entities. The end result will benefit the investor and help hedge funds compete with more traditional investments that, in today's investing marketplace, are more advantageous in this regard.

6. Improved Transparency

Today, institutional investors want and demand more transparency from hedge funds. Individual investors are no different. As competition for clients heats up, hedge funds will increase the disclosure of information to help win over clients. Regulators will most surely push for greater disclosure as well. Information that will see improved transparency includes assets under management, strategies followed, tools employed, and investment positions held. Full disclosure will not happen overnight, nor will disclosing the same level of information as mutual funds anytime soon. Rest assured, however, improved transparency is on the horizon.

7. Greater Use of Niche Strategies

As the number of hedge funds increases, the desire for hedge fund managers to set themselves apart will grow. One way to accomplish this aim will be to focus on one particular area or niche. Many managers are already doing this, but more will continue into the future. Today, many managers are already focusing on specific strategies such as macro-centric investing, fund of hedge funds, and merger arbitrage investing. The future will see these managers continue to become more specialized while including customized and unique tactics and techniques for profiting from opportunities. The result will be more niche managers who know their respective markets well and thus how to position their hedge funds for above normal profits and/or less risk.

8. Increase in the Number of Hedge Funds

With the future of hedge funds, nothing is a forgone conclusion. However, one trend that is most predictable is the continued growth in the number of hedge funds, both in the United States and abroad. Given the lure of significant compensation, less government oversight and regulation, and a reputation as a prized profession, hedge funds will continue to attract the best and the brightest from not only the traditional side of investing, but also from other professional careers that are not exactly related to investing. These people will come from legal, accounting, and marketing professions. Not only will new hedge fund management companies start from the ground up, but so too will the numbers of hedge funds grow at existing hedge fund companies. Low hurdles to entry will help to pave the way for ever increasing numbers of hedge funds. More hedge funds will equate to more options and opportunities for hedge fund investors.

9. Greater Geographic Diversification of Hedge Fund Managers

Today, the majority of hedge fund managers are located on the east coast of the United States, specifically New York and Connecticut. This will change. Over time, the diversification of hedge fund managers will rise as hedge funds open around the country and throughout the world. Money center cities such as Chicago, Charlotte, and San Francisco will experience much of the new diversification. Smaller cities and other major cities will also see new hedge funds established in their areas. This means greater accessibility to hedge fund managers for investors, which is usually a good thing.

10. Merging of Alternative and Traditional Managers

As hedge fund companies grow in size and complexity, so too will the services they offer. In doing so, hedge fund companies will start to look more and more like other traditional investment companies. Hedge fund companies will begin to offer more separate accounts, corresponding traditional investment accounts, trust establishment and management, and even tax planning. Many of these services are years away, but definitely on the horizon. The most sophisticated companies that want to attract more high-net worth investors will be most motivated and at the forefront of offering traditional services seen to be most interesting to this group of clients.

The hedge fund industry continues to change and mature. Over the next dozen years, factors such as increased competition, heightened governmental regulation, additional institutional involvement and pressure, and challenging market environments will help to transform the hedge fund trade into a more investor-friendly marketplace. This will attract more investments and open opportunities to the masses of investors.

Conclusion

Understanding Hedge Funds was written for those investors who want to allocate their portfolios properly for solid portfolio performance over the long-term. Hedge funds may be that missing component for many investors who are looking for an edge.

I hope you have enjoyed reading *Understanding Hedge Funds* and have learned how to invest in hedge funds with success. If you are interested in learning more about the *Journal of Asset Allocation* or how my firm can help protect and grow your wealth, please contact us for more information. In addition, please feel free to visit my official author web site for this book at www.UnderstandingHedgeFunds.com.

Scott Paul Frush, CFA, CFP, MBA   Voice: (248) 642-6800

Frush Financial Group   Email: Contact@Frush.com

37000 Woodward Avenue, Suite 101   Website: Frush.com

Bloomfield Hills, Michigan 48304

For more information on the basics of asset allocation and why allocating your portfolio is so important, I highly encourage you to read my book *Understanding Asset Allocation*, published by McGraw-Hill. *Understanding Asset Allocation* logically explains exactly what you need to know about how to allocate your assets. This comprehensive, highly accessible guide clearly explains the key principles of asset allocation, from selection to rebalancing to risk vs. return. You'll discover how the different asset classes behave, the leading misconceptions about asset allocation, and how risk profile, time horizon, and needs can impact your investments.

Be diligent and disciplined in your pursuit to create, grow and protect your wealth. All the very best on your endeavor to gain the investment *hEdge*.

Hedge Fund Resources

BOOKS:

Fundamentals of Hedge Fund Investing: A Professional Investor's Guide, by Bill Crerend ISBN 0070135223. An early book on hedge funds targeting intermediate to advanced investors who want to sharpen their hedge fund knowledge.

All About Hedge Funds: The Easy Way to Get Started, by Robert A. Jaeger ISBN 0071393935. One of the leading books on all things hedge funds. For the novice to intermediate investor.

Investing in Hedge Funds: An Investor's Guide, by Joseph G. Nicholas ISBN 1576601846. Nice introduction to hedge funds with emphasis on explaining hedge fund strategies.

Getting Started in Hedge Funds, by Daniel A. Strachman ISBN 0471715441. Good books on the basics of hedge funds. Targeted to novice investors.

Hedge Fund of Funds Investing: An Investor's Guide, by Joseph G. Nicholas ISBN 1576601242. Much emphasis is placed on fund of hedge funds. A good in-depth source.

A Random Walk Down Wall Street, by Burton G. Malkiel ISBN 0393325350. A time-honored book on investing and market behavior.

Evaluating Hedge Fund Performance, by Vinh Q. Tran ISBN 13978047681717. A good introductory book on hedge funds, with emphasis on picking the right hedge fund.

Understanding Asset Allocation, by Scott Frush ISBN 007147594X. Introduction to asset allocation, including how to build and grow a winning portfolio using asset allocation.

WEBSITES:

WSJ.com   A top source, if not the leading source, of broad financial and market information available. A must read on a daily basis.

HedgeWorld.com   For information on all things hedge fund related, this is one of the best resources.

Morningstar.com   A good source for the latest market news, investment analysis and financial happenings. From the company that assigns hedge fund rankings.

Finance.Yahoo.com   A personal favorite. An outstanding source for financial information. Covers both the depth and breadth of the market and market participants.

Bloomberg.com   Another of my personal favorites. A leading source of financial news and commentary.

HedgeFundCenter.com   Solid source of information and commentary on hedge funds.

DowJones.com   Provides an abundant source of historical information for the student of finance and investing. Top source for charting and historical prices.

UnderstandingHedgeFunds.com   This website is the official author website for this book. This site provides news, articles, books, and the latest updates with accolades received for *Understanding Hedge Funds*

PERIODICALS:

Wall Street Journal	*Financial Times*
Kiplinger's Personal Finance	*Fortune*
Barron's	*Forbes*
Money	*Red Herring*
The Economist	*Smart Money*

Mutual Funds   *Worth*
Bull & Bear Financial Report   *Business Week*
Journal of Alternative Investments

ASSOCIATIONS:

Alternative Investment Management
   Association (AIMA)   44-20-7659-9920
Meadows House, 20-22 Queen Street   www.aima.org
London W1J5PR
United Kingdom

Managed Funds Association   202-367-1140
2025 M Street N.W., Suite 800   www.mfainfo.org
Washington, D.C. 20036

Hedge Fund Association   202-478-2000
2875 N.E. 191st Street, Suite 900   www.thehfa.org
Aventura, FL 33180

Index

About the Author

Scott Paul Frush, CFA, CFP, is a leading authority on hedge funds and asset allocation policy. He is founder and president of Frush Financial Group, a wealth management firm in Bloomfield Hills, Michigan, and Trinity Catholic Funds, a hedge fund promoting catholic values investing. Frush is an accomplished financial advisor, a noted author, publisher of the *Journal of Asset Allocation*, and a consultant on asset allocation topics.

Frush has helped people protect, grow, and insure their wealth for more than a decade. In 2002, he founded the Frush Financial Group to manage portfolios for individuals, affluent families, and institutions using customized and sophisticated asset allocation solutions. Prior to founding his company, Frush worked at Jay A. Fishman Investment Counsel in Detroit, Michigan and Stein Roe Mutual Funds in Chicago, Illinois.

Frush earned his Master of Business Administration degree in finance from the University of Notre Dame and his Bachelor of Business Administration degree in finance from Eastern Michigan University. He holds the Chartered Financial Analyst (CFA) and Certified Financial Planner (CFP®) designations and is insurance licensed for life, health, property, and casualty. Frush is a member of the CFA Institute, Detroit Economic Club, National Association of Tax Professionals, and the Global Association of Risk Professionals.

Frush is the author of *Understanding Asset Allocation* (2006) and *Optimal Investing: How to Protect and Grow Your Wealth with Asset Allocation* (2004) - the recipient of two *Book of the Year* honors for business and investments. Frush has been quoted in or his work noted in over 50 publications across the United States.

The Frush Financial Group web site is www.Frush.com.